THE SONG OF SOLOMON COMPARED WITH OTHER PARTS OF SCRIPTURE

Published @ 2017 Trieste Publishing Pty Ltd

ISBN 9780649064496

The Song of Solomon Compared with Other Parts of Scripture by Solomon

Edited by Trieste Publishing Pty Ltd.
Cover @ 2017

www.triestepublishing.com

SOLOMON

THE SONG OF SOLOMON COMPARED WITH OTHER PARTS OF SCRIPTURE

Trieste

THE

SONG OF SOLOMON

COMPARED

WITH OTHER PARTS OF SCRIPTURE.

" Truly our fellowship is with the Father and with his Son Jesus
Christ."—1 John i. 3.

Second Edition.

LONDON:

JAMES NISBET AND CO., 21 BERNERS STREET.

MDCCCLII.

BALLANTYNE, PRINTER, EDINBURGH.

INTRODUCTORY THOUGHTS ON THE SONG OF SOLOMON.

" THE general character of this Book in contrast to Ecclesiastes is very striking. Ecclesiastes, from beginning to end, tells of the vanity of the creature—Canticles, of the sufficiency of the Beloved. In Ecclesiastes, the world is searched through and through in all its treasures of wisdom, of pleasure, and of riches ; but an object to satisfy the heart is not found in them all.

" All is vanity, yea, vanity of vanities !

" In Canticles, what a contrast ! An object to satisfy the heart is found ; that object is not the creature, but the Beloved. One verse in St John's Gospel gives the contrast perfectly (John iv. 14). Ecclesiastes is the first half of the verse—' Whosoever drinketh of this water *shall thirst again ;*' Canticles is the latter half of the verse—' Whosoever drinketh of the water that I shall give him *shall never thirst.*' '*His love*' is better than wine, than riches, than treasures, than all things."—EXTRACT.

Thus the Book is *full of Jesus.* But it is Jesus in a peculiar character. He is not seen here as " Saviour," nor as " King," nor as " High Priest," nor as " Judge," nor as " Prophet," nor as " the Captain of our Salvation," nor as " the Great Shepherd of the sheep," nor as " the Mighty God," nor as " the King of kings," nor as his people's " Surety" —No! it is in a dearer and closer relation than any of these—it is Jesus as our " Bridegroom "—Jesus in marriage union with his Bride, his Church.

This is a great mystery, but it is one of most peculiar preciousness to " all them that *love* our Lord Jesus Christ in sincerity." It pervades every part of Holy Scripture. It was first revealed in Adam and Eve, in Eden (Gen. i. 27, and ii. 21-24). It was more fully brought out in the typical characters of the Old Testament ; as, for example, in Boaz and Ruth ; it was distinctly taught in the betrothment of the Jewish nation ; and it is plainly declared in the spiritual language of the epistles—" I have espoused you *to one husband,* that I may present you as a chaste virgin *to Christ*" (2 Cor. xi. 2).

The Song of Solomon is to be understood as the mutual interchange of the affections of the Bridegroom and the Bride. It is the experience of the soul towards Christ in this peculiar relationship.

We may be quite *as safe*, though we realise our interest in Christ *only* as our Saviour from the guilt and condemnation of sin; or if we know him only one step further, as the Captain of our Salvation, making us more than conquerors in fighting the good fight of faith. But it is our privilege (*and a great one*) to know him in a world that passeth away, wherein we are but strangers and pilgrims, *ever learning the bitterness of creature-disappointments, and the drying up of creature-streams of happiness*—as *the one object* in whom our affections may supremely centre with no danger of excess, no fear of disappointment, no possibility of coolness or variableness in return; but rather, *in whose love* we shall meet with a response that shall make *our* love as *nothing*, by reason of *the love that excelleth!*

This is our privilege—a purchased privilege—ours in virtue of our relationship in Jesus.

The question is never once raised throughout the Book whether indeed it is so or not. Grief and sadness arise from other causes. For, as the one grand aim of the Bride throughout is the enjoyment of free, uninterrupted, and constant *communion* with the Beloved, so the grand source of sorrow and distress is when seasons of coldness, lukewarmness, and drowsiness ever and anon creep over the soul, coming

between it and Jesus, like clouds which hide the sun
—not, indeed, affecting *its* bright shining, but effectually hindering the genial warmth of its cheering,
enlightening, and life-giving rays from reaching the
soul.

One of the most striking features of this Book is
the development of the onward, ripening progress of
Christian experience, as traced through the spring,
summer, and autumnal seasons (chap. ii., iv., and
vi.) " First the blade, then the ear ; after that the
full corn in the ear."

And one of its most prominent characteristics is,
that THE PERSON of Christ is dwelt on, rather than
his work and offices. He is loved, so to speak, *for
his own sake.* It is *" his own self"* that is the much-
loved object.

May our affections more and more centre in
Jesus ; and may he be the constant companion and
friend of our otherwise desolate and unsatisfied
hearts, " until the day break and the shadows flee
away," and " the marriage of the Lamb" be *come!*

CONTENTS.

THE SONG OF SOLOMON

COMPARED WITH OTHER PARTS OF SCRIPTURE.

"This is a great mystery; but I speak concerning Christ and the Church."—EPH. v. 27.

CHAPTER I.

Ver. 1. *" The Song of songs, which is Solomon's."*

" LET the word of Christ dwell in you richly in all wisdom, teaching and admonishing one another in psalms and hymns and *spiritual songs, singing with grace in your hearts* unto the Lord " (Col. iii. 16; Eph. v. 19). " For it is a good thing . . . to *sing praises* unto thy name, O most High " (Ps. xcii. 1–3; lxxxix. 1).

It was thus that *Moses* sang, to celebrate the exodus and redemption of Israel from the land of Egypt (Ex. xv.) It was thus that *Deborah* sang, to celebrate the victory of Barak over Sisera (Judges v.)

It was thus *David* sang, " in the day that God delivered him out of the hand of all his enemies " (2 Sam. xxii.)   It was thus that *Paul* and *Silas*, even in the prison, " sang praises unto God " at midnight (Acts xvi.)   Israel shall, in like manner, sing " in the land of Judah " the song that is prepared for them in the coming day of their restoration (Isa. xxvi.)

And yet all these are but foretastes of the heavenly song which shall be sung by the redeemed out of " all nations, and kindreds, and peoples, and tongues " (Rev. v. 9, &c.)—" a new song "—" the song of the Lamb ! " (Rev. xiv. 4, and xv. 2-4.)

The heavenly song will be sung by the Church of Christ *in glory;* " the Song of songs, which is Solomon's," is the song they sing here *upon earth.*

Pre-eminence is given to it above every other, when it is called " the Song of songs," which double rendering is very emphatic in the Hebrew.   Thus Jehovah is called the " God of gods and Lord of lords " (Deut. x. 17) ; and Christ is called " King of kings and Lord of lords " (Rev. xix. 16).   So also the " most holy place " is called " the holy of holies," signifying that it was the treasury of the highest and most sacred mysteries of God.   And St Paul has explained to us how great is the mystery contained in this " Song of songs," when he declares, " *for this cause* shall a man leave his father and mother, and shall be joined unto his wife, and they two shall be one flesh.   This is a great mystery ;

but I speak concerning Christ and the Church" (Eph.
v. 29–32).

The mystic union is involved in the attributing
of the song to Solomon ; for it is uttered mutually
by Christ and by his Church, but it is attributed to
him only, for they are not twain, but one. And she
is lost sight of in him. The same Spirit actuates
both ; for the Head and the members form *but one
Christ.* The song is, therefore, emphatically " Solomon's," or *Christ's.*

The Bride.

Ver. 2. " *Let him kiss me with the kisses of his mouth.*"

This abrupt commencement bespeaks the impas-
sioned affections of the Bride. She is so wholly
engrossed with thoughts of her Beloved, that she
does not stay to explain of whom she speaks. Just
as Mary at the sepulchre, looking for Jesus, ad-
dressed herself to one whom she believed to be the
gardener, exclaiming, " If thou have borne *him* hence,
tell me where thou hast laid him, and I will take
him away "—as though every one must know *whom*
she sought (John xx. 15)—as though there were
but one object to be cared for—*One* for whom she
would count all things else but loss (Phil. iii. 7, 8) ;
and *one* pearl of great price, to buy which she would
sell all that she had (Matt. xiii. 44–46). For,
" Whom have I in heaven *but thee ?* and there is

none upon earth that I desire *beside thee*," must ever be the language of *the Bride* of Christ.

" Let him kiss me." A kiss is a token of very near and intimate friendship, or of relationship. It, therefore, bespeaks, in this instance, the intimacy and closeness of the relationship between Jesus and his Church. We have a striking representation of it in the case of David and Jonathan, in 1 Sam. xx. 41 : " They kissed one another, and wept one with another, until David exceeded."

But a kiss is also a token of reconciliation, which we have beautifully brought before us in the Prodigal Son returning to his father's house :— " When he was yet a great way off, his father saw him, and had compassion, and ran, and fell on his neck, and *kissed him*," &c. (Luke xv. 20). And a similar instance of reconciliation occurs in the history of Joseph, who, in making himself known to them, " *kissed* all his brethren, and wept upon them : and after that, his brethren talked with him " (Gen. xlv. 15). " God was in Christ, *reconciling* the world unto himself" (2 Cor. v. 18–21 ; Rom. v. 10, 11 ; Col. i. 21 ; Heb. ii. 17).

" With the kisses *of his mouth ;*" for " his mouth is most sweet " (Cant. v. 16) ; " Neither was guile found in his mouth ;" " All bare him witness, and wondered at the gracious words which proceeded out of his mouth " (Luke iv. 22 ; 1 Pet. ii. 22 ; Matt. iv. 4). And, therefore, Job declares : " I have esteemed the words *of his* mouth more than my necessary food " (Job xxiii. 12).

Contrast " *his* mouth" with *ours* (James iii. 2–10).

" *For thy love is better than wine.*"

" *Thy* love"—the love of Jesus—truly it is sweet. Very tender is the love between the Husband and his Bride ; therefore she exclaims, " Let him kiss me with the kisses of his mouth." Dearer is such love than the choicest earthly good—more refreshing, more reviving, more strengthening. It is " an everlasting love" (Jer. xxxi. 3). " Having loved his own which were in the world, he loved them unto the end" (John xiii. 1). How unlike a mere earthly passion, producing a sudden flash of excitement, and dying away again ! " Thy love is better than wine " —" Thy loving-kindness is better than life" (Ps. lxiii. 3). Oh! to comprehend more of "the breadth, and length, and depth, and height, and to know the love of Christ which passeth knowledge ! " " Greater love hath no man." It was love " strong as death" (John xv. 13 ; Cant. viii. 6). It was the very same love as that wherewith the Father loved the Son !—" *as* the Father hath loved me, *so* have I loved you" (John xv. 9). Well, therefore, may we exclaim with David, " How excellent is thy loving-kindness, O God !" for "thou shalt make them *drink of the river* of thy pleasures" (Ps. xxxvi. 7–10), an exhaustless stream—" BETTER than wine ! "

Ver. 3. *" Because of the savour of thy good ointments, thy name is as ointment poured forth."*

When Mary brake the box of ointment of spikenard, very costly, we read that " the house was filled
with the odour of the ointment" (John xii. 3). It
is thus when the " name" of Jehovah is revealed :
" thy name is as ointment *poured forth."*

For God's name is *the expression* of his nature,
character, and attributes, as we may learn from the
proclamation of it to Moses (Ex. xxxiv. 5–7). But
it is essentially Jesus : " thou shalt call his name
Emmanuel, which, being interpreted, is, God with
us" (Matt. i. 23); *in him* the ointment is " poured
forth," the name of God is exhibited ; and whereso-
ever Jesus comes, the place is filled with the sweet
odour of " the name" of our God. Thus it is
written, " The Word was made flesh, and dwelt
among us, and *we beheld* his glory ;" there was, as it
were, the breaking of the box, that the ointment
might be " poured forth." God revealed his name
in the person of his dear Son (Isa. vii. 14 ; ix. 6).

It is compared to ointment because it was

1. Most precious and costly (Ex. xxx. 23–25 ; Ps.
   cxxxiii. 2 ; Mark xiv. 3 ; John xii. 3; 1 Pet.
   ii. 7). " Unto you, therefore, which believe, he
   is precious."
2. Of sweet odour (Eph. v. 2). " Christ also hath
   loved us, and hath given himself for us, an
   offering and a sacrifice to God, for a sweet-
   smelling savour" (John xii. 3).

3. Compounded of a variety of parts (Ex. xxx.
23–28). " It pleased the Father that *in him*
should *all fulness* dwell" (Col. i. 19 ; ii. 9).
4. It had healing properties (Acts iii. 16). " His
name, through faith in his name, hath made
this man strong."
Lastly, Nothing was ever to be made like it (Ex.
xxx. 31–33, 37, 38). " There is none other
name under heaven given among men whereby
we must be saved" (Acts iv. 12).

" Therefore do the virgins love thee."

It is as the Father is *known* in the person of
Christ that he is loved. " This is life eternal, to
know thee, the only true God, and *Jesus Christ,*
whom thou hast sent" (John xvii. 3). Because in
Jesus there is such a full manifestation and exhibi-
tion of the character and name of God, like ointment
poured forth, "*therefore* do the virgins love thee."
(Compare 1 John iv. 9, 19.) " We love him because he first loved us." (See also Luke vii. 47.)

" The virgins" are so called for their spiritual
chastity. " That I may present you as a *chaste
virgin* to Christ" (2 Cor. xi. 3). The same word is
rendered "thy hidden ones," in Ps. lxxxiii. 3.

Ver. 4. *Draw me, we will run after thee."*

The word " draw " rather signifies precede, or go
before me. Thus we should follow Jesus as our
" forerunner," who has gone before, " leaving us an

example, that we should follow his steps" (1 Pet. i. 21. See Heb. vi. 20).

The prayer implies a sense of helplessness—"*draw me* ;" it implies also a looking to God for the needed help—"Mine eyes are ever towards the Lord," &c. (Ps. xxv. 15). "Send out *thy* light and *thy* truth ; let them *lead* me, let them *bring* me," &c. (Ps. xliii. 3). It further implies a sense of restlessness at a distance from God, and an earnest desire for closer communion with him : "It is *good* for me to *draw near* unto God" (Ps. lxxiii. 28).

"Draw me." And how truly the God of our mercy *does* "prevent" us ! (Ps. lix. 10.) "I drew them with cords of a man, with bands of love ;" "With loving-kindness have I drawn thee" (Hos. xi. 4 ; Jer. xxxi. 3). So again, in Deut. i. 33, "Who went in the way *before you*," &c. It is his own promise, "I, if I be lifted up from the earth, will draw all men unto me" (John xii. 32). And yet the necessity for the prayer is evident, for that he hath also said, "No man can come unto me, except the Father which hath sent me draw him" (John vi. 44). But wherever the cry is sincere, it is a sure earnest of the Spirit in the heart already ; and *we know* that whatsoever we ask according to his will, or according to the intercession of the Spirit in us, he will give it us (1 John v. 13, 14). And the soul appears to realise this, being quickened in the lively exercise of faith, even whilst in the very act of prayer. For, instead of inertness, the following words suggest the idea of more than ordinary activity—"Draw me, we will *run* after thee."

It expresses something of the energetic spirit of Peter, in John xxi. 7, who, as soon as he heard that it was the Lord, "cast himself into the sea," as though he could not soon enough find himself at his Lord's feet. He was unable to restrain his ardent love whilst they drew the ship to land.

Thus David also says, "I will *run* in the way of thy commandments when thou shalt enlarge my heart" (Ps. cxix. 32); and, again, "I *made haste*, and delayed not," &c. (ver. 60). And St Paul says, "This one thing I do, forgetting the things which are behind, and *reaching forth* unto those things which are before, I *press* toward the mark," &c. (Phil. iii. 13, 14).

We have likewise the word of exhortation—"*so run* that ye may obtain" (1 Cor. ix. 24, 25). "Let us run with patience *the race* that is set before us" (Heb. xii. 1, 2). "Not slothful in business, but *fervent* in spirit" (Rom. xii. 11). And there is a precious promise and word of encouragement in Isa. xl. 31, "They that wait upon the Lord shall renew their strength: they shall mount up with wings as eagles; they shall *run* and not be weary, and they shall walk and not faint."

Only we must see that we "*run after*" our Lord, and not *before* him; that is, not marking out for ourselves a way of our own, but treading *in His steps.* "When he putteth forth his own sheep, *he goeth before them,* and the sheep *follow him*" (John x. 4, 5, 27).

" The King hath brought me into his chambers."

The prayer is answered, and answered in God's own way, far exceeding even our own desires. We are permitted not only to follow after, but *to enter in* with our Beloved to his royal chambers! Here is the soul *" entering into the holiest* by the blood of Jesus," having access *within* the *vail* (Heb. x. 19, 20). For, by virtue of our marriage union with Jesus, we are "kings and priests." " He hath made us sit together *in heavenly places* in Christ Jesus" (Eph. ii. 6), being " of the household of God" (ii. 19) ; and it is our amazing privilege to dwell " in the secret place of the Most High" (Ps. xci. 1 ; xxvii. 4, 5 ; lxv. 4). " Blessed is the man whom thou choosest, and causest to *approach* unto *thee,* that he may dwell *in thy courts,*" &c. Surely it is here that Jesus manifests himself unto us as he doth not unto the world (John xiv. 18, 23). And it is here we taste the sweet anticipations of being hereafter admitted into the " many mansions" of the " Father's house," in glory (John xiv. 3). We are now, as it were, abiding for a season in *the ante-chamber* through faith ; but Jesus is preparing a place for us, when the earthly house (or *hut*) of this tabernacle is dissolved, where we shall sit down with him in his throne, and reign for ever and ever in the royal presence chamber of our King! "They shall *see his face*, ... and they shall reign for ever and ever" (Rev. iii. 21; 2 Cor. v. 1; Rev. xxii. 4, 5). "They shall enter into the King's palace!" (Ps. xlv. 16.)

Jesus is seen as the Priest (in ver. 3), seated on his *throne* as "the King" (in ver. 4), for he is our Melchizedec, our royal High Priest, in the temple made without hands.

"*We will be glad and rejoice in thee.*"

There is here the *inward feeling* and the *outward expression* of joy. The gladness is the same as in Ps. civ. 34, "My meditation of him shall be sweet. I will be glad in the Lord"—a joy in the inmost recesses of the soul—"My *heart* is glad" (Ps. xvi. 9). So the *rejoicing* is the outward manifestation of it, "and my glory rejoiceth" (Ps. xvi. 9). These two commonly go together;—"My *soul* shall make her boast in the Lord;" there is the inward feeling: "the humble shall *hear thereof* and be glad;" there is the outward manifestation of it (Ps. xxxiv. 2; xxxiii. 1). But it is all "*in thee*".—"in the Lord." "I will greatly rejoice *in the Lord*; my soul shall be joyful *in my* God" (Isa. lxi. 10; Hab. iii. 17, 18; 1 Sam. ii. 1; Phil. iv. 1, 4). If we rejoice at any time in frames and feelings, in earthly prosperity, or in spiritual welfare (see Ps. xxx. 6, 7), it cannot be abiding joy. "Rejoice in the Lord alway," for in him there is "alway" cause of rejoic-

ing, but in none else. We should seek to share
Jesus' joy: "that they might have *my* joy fulfilled
in themselves" (John xvii. 13).

" We will remember thy love more than wine."

"There be many that say, Who will shew us any
good? Lord, lift thou up the light of *thy* countenance upon us. For *thou* hast put gladness in my
heart, more than in the time that their corn and
their wine increased" (Ps. iv. 6, 7).

The believer feels that the Lord's love is "more
to be desired than gold, yea, than much fine gold,
sweeter also than honey and the honeycomb."
Thus he can rejoice in the love of his God, "though
the fig-tree shall not blossom, neither shall fruit be
in the vine," &c. (Hab. iii. 17, 18). He has a
fountain of living waters to draw from, therefore he
needs not to go to the well for water; earthly
treasures can no longer charm him. "If a man
would give all the substance of his house *for love,*
it would utterly be contemned" (Cant. viii. 7).
"We will remember *thy love* more than wine."

But the term "remember" implies past experience
looked back upon; it is *contemplation,* and not seeking for some new thing: "I remember the days of
old," &c. (Ps. cxliii. 5; lxiii. 6; lxxvii. 10, 11).

The Lord's Supper is a special act of remembrance.
"Do this *in remembrance* of me." "To the end that
we should alway remember the exceeding great love
of our Master and only Saviour, Jesus Christ, thus

dying for us . . . . he hath instituted and ordained
holy mysteries as pledges of his love, and for a continual remembrance of his death, to our great and
endless comfort." It is a most precious ordinance
for the strengthening and refreshing of the soul, as
the body is refreshed by the bread and wine.

" *The upright love thee.*"

" Let love be without dissimulation" (Rom. xii.
9). There must be integrity and *whole-heartedness*,
where there is true love to the Lord Jesus. Not
"a heart and a heart," for we cannot love God and
Mammon. Is it not so even among men, that if
any man will marry, our Church inquires, " Wilt
thou love her, comfort her, &c. ; and, *forsaking all
other*, keep thee *only* unto her ?" &c. And how
much *more*, then, when we are espoused to the Lord
Jesus Christ ! Very great is the blessedness of integrity and uprightness. " No good thing will he
withhold from them *that walk uprightly*" (Ps.
lxxxiv. 11). " The integrity of the upright shall
guide them " (Prov. xi. 3). Oh, for grace to be able
at all times to say with an *upright* heart, " Lord,
thou knowest all things, thou knowest that I love
thee"! (John xxi. 17.)

Ver. 5. " *I am black, but comely, O ye daughters of
Jerusalem, as the tents of Kedar, as the curtains of
Solomon.*"

The contemplation of uprightness seems to have

turned the thoughts of the Bride aside for a moment, to reply to some who appear to have charged or suspected her of a different character. These "daughters of Jerusalem" are frequently mentioned throughout the book, and may, most probably, represent *professors*; those who compose a part of the visible, but not the true, Church of Christ on earth. They are "daughters of Jerusalem," but they are *not* "the *Bride*—the Lamb's *Wife*." They partake of the outward privileges, but they know not the vital union of the Bride with her Beloved; and, therefore, they fail to understand much of her experience.

She therefore unfolds to them here one of the fundamental truths of Christianity—the utter blackness of the child of God *in himself*, together with his completeness and beauty in *Christ*. " I am black, but comely." " I am black"—here is the full acknowledgment of her state by nature. "Behold, I was shapen in iniquity, and in sin did my mother conceive me" (Ps. li. 5 ; Rom. iii. 10, &c. ; Jer. xvii. 9 ; Gen. viii. 21 ; Mark vii. 21, 23, &c. &c.)

And even after conversion, it is equally true of us, as it was of St Paul, " For I know that in me (that is, in my flesh) dwelleth *no* good thing " (Rom. vii. 18 ; see also Isa. vi. 5).

And it appears to be in this latter sense that the expression is intended here ; for the original word is literally " *dark* " as the dawn of day, justly representing the state of the Church of Christ on earth, emerging, as it were, from the ruins of the tomb, from a death in trespasses and sins, but awaiting the light of day in the morning of the Resurrection.

None are so ready to say of themselves, " I am black," as the most advanced Christians. St Paul had been one for *thirty years* when he declared himself the chief of sinners (1 Tim. i. 15) ; and the better we know ourselves, the more deeply we feel, "*I am black.*"

" Black—as the tents of Kedar." There is great force in this illustration. " The tents of the Arabs are of a dark or nearly black colour, being made of the shaggy hair of their black goats." And what could be a fitter representation of the Church of Christ in the eyes of the world ? " Hath not God chosen *the poor* of this world, rich in faith, and heirs of the kingdom ?" (James ii. 5.)

> " Poor and afflicted, Lord, are thine,
> Among the great they seldom shine."

They have nothing to render them *outwardly* attractive—to the eye of sense they are " as the tents of Kedar." They have no earthly *city* to dwell in— they are literally " strangers and pilgrims " on the earth, sojourning in " *tents,*" and content with the traveller's fare, for they seek a city.

But if destitute of *exterior* beauty, like the Arab tents, they are richly adorned *within,* " as the curtains of Solomon " (1 Pet. iii. 4). None saw the exquisite loveliness of those curtains, save those who entered *within* the tabernacle or temple. Even Jesus was " without form or comeliness" to those who looked only on his outward lowly garb of suffering humanity. But his Bride discovered such charms in her Beloved, that, at a loss for words to express it, she exclaimed, "Yea, he is altogether lovely!"

And it is in *his* comeliness *she* is comely. "I am black, but comely"—"Perfect through *my* comeliness which I had *put upon thee*, saith the Lord God" (Ezek. xvi. 14).

Precious truth! Without one of the filthy rags of their own righteousness, they are "covered with the robe of his righteousness," and "clothed with the garments of salvation" (Isa. lxi. 10)—"Accepted in the beloved" (Eph. i. 7)—"Perfect in Christ Jesus" (Col. i. 28)—Yea, "*complete in him*" (Col. ii. 10). "I am black but comely."

> " Since, therefore, I can hardly bear
> What in myself I see,
> How vile, *how black*, must I appear,
> Most Holy God, to thee!
> But, oh! my Saviour stands between,
> In garments dyed in blood :
> 'Tis *He* instead of me is seen,
> When I approach to God."—NEWTON.

Ver. 6. "*Look not upon me, because I am black, because the sun hath looked upon me: my mother's children were angry with me; they made me keeper of the vineyards, but mine own vineyard have I not kept.*"

The offence of the Cross has not ceased. "All that will live godly in Christ Jesus shall suffer persecution" (2 Tim. iii. 12).—"In the world ye shall have tribulation" (John xvi. 33; see also John xvii. 14; John xv. 19; 1 John iii. 13).

Nay more, "A man's foes shall be they *of his own household*" (Matt. x. 36; Mic. vii. 6)—"My mother's children were angry with me." And there is no persecution so hard as this, arising not from avowed enemies, but from professed friends or relatives.

A large part of Job's trial arose from it; he was misunderstood and bitterly reproached by his own friends. And it has been truly remarked that " Moses knew the trial of *the camp*, even beyond that of *the wilderness*." To be looked down upon by fellow-Christians (or those professing to be such), is indeed an arrow that pierces the heart very keenly.

But it is a great sin to despise one of the Lord's little ones (Matt. xviii. 10). The judgments on Edom were very sore and terrible, for having thus lightly esteemed his brother Jacob. "Thou shouldest not have looked upon the day of thy brother, in the day that he became a stranger; yea, thou shouldest not have looked on their affliction in the day of their calamity," &c. (Obad. 12, 13, &c.)

Yet the Lord oft-times turns this day of affliction into a day of blessing to his people, inasmuch as it leads them to self-conviction of grievous shortcoming, and the many times in which they have "given occasion to the enemies of the Lord to blaspheme." " Mine own vineyard have I not kept."

Ver. 7. *" Tell me, O thou whom my soul loveth,
where thou feedest, where thou makest thy flock to
rest at noon; for why should I be as one that
turneth aside by the flocks of thy companions?"*

The Bride soon returns to address herself *to her
Beloved;* and we have in these words a full turning
of the heart to Jesus, in whom the soul alone finds
rest, when all others are against her. The cry
seems to arise *out of solitude of experience;* for none
else could understand or sympathise with her. By
the flocks of his companions she was *as one veiled*
(see marg.) *They* could not read the secrets of her
heart, but *he* could ; and in full confidence of heart
she appeals to him—" Tell me, O thou whom my
soul loveth."

Here was the strongest evidence of her uprightness—" The upright love thee ; " and in full consciousness of the love she bore to him, she turns
directly *to him* as the Searcher of hearts, who knew
what others could not know of the longings of her
inmost soul.

This is precious experience, and it is well to be
brought to it by any means. " The sun," saith she,
" hath looked upon me—I am faint and languishing
—O tell me where I may find rest in those green
pastures, and beside those still waters, where thou
makest thy flock to rest at noon! for *why* should I be
as one that turneth aside?" &c. Oh ! how often
believers are heard to speak thus ! *Why* cannot I
enjoy the rich provisions of covenant love as others

do ? Why am I cut off from a participation in the means of grace, or from enjoyment in them ? "Why go I mourning all my days because of the oppression of the enemy !" (Ps. xlii. 9.) "O tell me *where* thou feedest thy flock, and where thou causest them to lie down," &c. (Ezek. xxxiv.) "Shew me thy ways, O Lord, teach me thy paths" (Ps. xxv. 4, 5).

This should ever be the language of *the wandering sheep*. "Seek thy servant, for I do not forget thy commandments" (Ps. cxix. 176). And that it was but a wandering sheep, a sheep that had only *strayed* from the fold, is evident ; for none but a true member of Christ's flock could have urged that plea, "O thou whom my soul loveth."

Sad it is, but too true, that the Lord's people are prone to wander. And yet (blessed be God !) they find no rest *away* from him. Having once known the Lord as their "Good Shepherd," they will never find satisfaction in any other pasture (Ps. xxiii. 1, &c.; John x. 5 ; see also 1 John iv. 1–4).

The Lord's Answer.

Ver. 8. "*If thou know not, O thou fairest among women, go thy way forth by the footsteps of the flock, and feed thy kids by the shepherds' tents.*"

There is no upbraiding with our God. If at any time we lack wisdom, we may ask it of him, for he giveth to all men liberally (James i. 5).

"*If* thou know not"—the words almost imply

that there *was* the knowledge, though not in exercise. As in John xiv. 8, 9, "Have I been so long time with you, and yet hast thou not known me, Philip?" How is it that ye know not? "Thus saith the Lord, Stand ye *in the way*, and see, and ask *for the old paths*, where is the good way, and walk therein; and ye shall find rest unto your souls" (Jer. vi. 16). "*I* am the way," saith Jesus. Follow the leading of the Good Shepherd, and tread in the footsteps of his flock, for "*they follow him.*" Therefore, "be followers of *them*," &c. (Heb. vi. 12; 1 Cor. xi. 1; 1 Thess. i. 6; Heb. xiii. 7; Phil. iii. 16, 17). "Forsake not the assembling of yourselves together;" for, "Where two or three are gathered together in my name, *there am I* in the midst of them" (Heb. x. 25; Matt. xxviii. 19, 20).

Be diligent in the use of means; "feed thy kids," &c. It seems as if the Lord would say, "Indulge not in thy feelings of lonely desolateness; withdraw not thyself from thy fellow-Christians—the Shepherd is with his flock; and, if thou wouldest find *him*, abide with *them*."

Ver. 9. "*I have compared thee, O my love, to a company of horses in Pharaoh's chariot.*"

So far from casting reproach upon his Bride, the Lord encourages her with words of tenderness and delight, in a figure most fitly representing her condition while militant here upon earth—"a company of horses in Pharaoh's chariot." And in this and the two following verses, he strikingly contrasts *his* estimation of her strength, activity, and swiftness, and her exceeding beauty, with her own sense of feebleness and acknowledgment of blackness expressed in verses 4–6.

Believers may be compared to Pharaoh's horses in that they were very choice and costly (see 1 Kings x. 29). For we are "a *chosen* generation," and "*purchased*" with the inestimable price of "the precious blood of Christ."

There is remarkable beauty in this figure, when taken in connexion with Solomon's history; it is stated, in proof of his amazing wealth, that "Solomon had horses *brought out of Egypt*—and they fetched up, and brought forth out of Egypt, a chariot for six hundred shekels of silver, and a horse for an hundred and fifty" (2 Chron. i. 16, 17). It is a very beautiful figurative representation of the true Solomon redeeming his people, at an infinitely higher cost, "out of the land of Egypt, out of the house of bondage." And it gives a peculiar propriety to the selection of *this* as the first figure chosen by the Lord in which to address his Bride, calling vividly to remembrance whence she was brought; for he would ever have us humbled under the recollection of "the rock whence we are hewn, and *the hole of the pit* whence we are digged" (Isa. li. 1).

Ver. 10, 11. "*Thy cheeks are comely with rows of*

*jewels, thy neck with chains of gold.   We will
make thee borders of gold, with studs of silver."*

The Lord takes pleasure in *beautifying* the meek,
and in adorning his Bride (Ps. cxlix. 4).   The
word " *We* " is the same as that used in Gen. i. 26,
which involves the three Persons of the Godhead.
As they created, so they *new* create and " beautify."
Thus Isaiah says of the Lord—" He hath covered
me with the robe of righteousness, as a bridegroom
decketh himself with ornaments, and as a bride
adorneth herself with jewels " (Isa. lxi. 10).

And the Lord himself declares of Jerusalem, that
when he entered into covenant with her and she became his, he *decked* her also with ornaments, and
put bracelets on her hands, and a chain on her neck,
&c. (Ezek. xvi. 11, 12.)   And then he adds, " Thus
wast thou decked with silver and gold."—" Borders
of gold, with studs of silver."

Chains of gold about the neck were always tokens
of promotion ; as, when Pharaoh promoted Joseph,
" He arrayed him in fine linen, and put a gold chain
about his neck " (Gen. xli. 41, 42) ; and when
Daniel was promoted by Belshazzar to be the third
ruler in his kingdom, he also clothed him with
" scarlet, and put a chain of gold about his neck "
(Dan. v. 29).   But our adorning is not to be of
"gold, or pearls, or costly array—but in good works "
(1 Tim. ii. 9, 10).

THE BRIDE.

Ver. 12. " While the King sitteth at his table, my spikenard sendeth forth the smell thereof."

Here is the royal Bride promoted to the highest dignity, "seated beside the King," at his royal feast, yet "clothed with humility."

"The King sitteth at his table." Once the King of glory, veiled in human flesh, headed the table at which sat his twelve apostles, when he instituted that precious ordinance in which we commemorate his dying love; nor is he less present with us now in the Gospel Feast—"Where two or three are gathered together in my name, *there am I* in the midst."

He "sitteth at his table." How sweet to remember that the feast is *his!* The table is "his!"—the provisions are his !—and the guests are his ! Boasting, therefore, is excluded, for it is all of grace, and the Bride may humbly *own* the fragrance of her spikenard—"My spikenard sendeth forth the smell thereof." It is in seasons of communion with the Lord that the graces of the Spirit are called forth in most lively exercise—" *While* the King sitteth at his table." When the presence of Christ is realised, then do love, gratitude, humility, faith, gentleness, meekness, &c. &c., flow forth in sweetest fragrance towards *their Author.* The *spirit* of the Bride (intimated by the *spikenard* sending forth its smell) is

beautifully expressed in our Communion Service:
" We do not *presume* to come to this *thy table*, O
Lord, trusting in our own righteousness, but in thy
manifold and great mercies. We are not worthy so
much as to gather up the crumbs under thy table,
but," &c. For the " spikenard " is a lowly grass,
scarcely rising above the surface of the ground. A
lovely emblem of humility. And being admitted
into the royal presence, and even sitting down to the
same royal feast with Jesus the King of kings, does
not foster pride, but deepens humility. What, indeed, could so effectually cherish a lowly spirit at
this feast, as the remembrance of the Saviour's words,
that at his coming again, " he shall gird himself,
and make them (his servants) to come and sit down
to meat, and shall come forth and serve *them* " ? (Luke
xii. 37.)

Is it not strange that any can leave this same
Jesus knocking without at the door of their hearts,
when he has said that if any man will open the door,
he will come in to him, and *sup with him?* (Rev. iii.
20.) Alas ! that any should reject that wedding-
garment in which alone they can appear at " his
table " ! (Mat. xxii. 10, 12.)

It is too precious a thought to the children of God
to be forgotten here, that the Captain of their salvation does not leave them without provisions in their
enemies' land, whilst they are engaged in fighting
the good fight of faith ; for it is written, " Thou
preparest a table before me in the presence of mine

enemies" (Ps. xxiii. 5). Even there their King is in the midst of them, and "sitteth at his table."

Ver. 13. *"A bundle of myrrh is my well-beloved unto me: he shall lie all night betwixt my breasts."*

So precious are the seasons of communion with her "well-beloved," that his Bride resolves upon unbroken intimacy of the closest kind.

"A bundle of myrrh" is he unto me! "Myrrh" was one of the choice spices of the East. "A bundle" of it would therefore bespeak great treasures, and rich abundance of them. Yet the figure but faintly pourtrays *the fulness* that is treasured up for us in Christ Jesus. "For in him dwelleth all the fulness of the Godhead bodily" (Col. ii. 9). "The only be-gotten of the Father, *full* of grace and truth" (John i. 14.) "All fulness dwells in him."

And he is all this to each of his people : "A bundle of myrrh is *my* well-beloved unto *me*." When the soul is so enamoured with the loveliness of Jesus as to call him in all sincerity "my *well-beloved*," we need not wonder at the strength of her appropriating faith. She felt how much she loved him. How could she question whether he was *her* beloved ?

"My *well*-beloved !" "Unto you which believe he is *precious*" (1 Pet. ii. 7). He has become the one supreme object of your affections ; you can say, "There is none upon earth I desire *beside thee*." No creature-idol shall share *his* place in your heart. The

Bride of Jesus ought indeed to seek after no other lovers; none should have any *share* in her affections. At all times she ought to be able to say, " *He* shall lie all night betwixt my breasts." But, alas! how often believers have to mourn over a "divided heart"! and even when bereft of one idol, how they turn to another, and yet another! As in Ezek. xvi. 15, 30, that chapter which gives us such a picture of the return we make for God's love to us; or, as it is written in Jer. iii. 1, "thou hast played the harlot with *many* lovers;" our hearts running after one and another whom we love, alas! better than Jesus.

And yet, so unalterable, so unchanging are *His* affections towards us, that he says, " YET return *again* to me, saith the Lord!" " Let her, therefore, put away her whoredoms out of her sight, and her adulteries *from between her breasts*," &c., and I my-self will constrain her to return to me. For " behold, I will hedge up thy way with thorns, and make a way that she shall not find her paths. And she shall follow after her lovers, but she shall not overtake them," &c.; " *then* shall she say, I will go and return to my first husband. And it shall be, in that day, saith the Lord, that thou shalt call me Ishi (that is, 'my husband'), and I will betroth thee *unto me* for *ever!*" (see Hos. ii. 2, &c.) What amazing love! what marvellous forbearance! what comfort to the wretched adulteress, who, after the manner of men, imagines that Jesus can never love such an one again! But he will *never* cast thee off, though thou hast wronged him thus. He has entered into covenant with thee, and though thou has broken "*thy* covenant," he says, "*nevertheless*, I will remember *my* covenant with thee in the day of thy youth, and I will establish unto thee an everlasting covenant" (Ezek. xvi. 60, 62); and he undertakes *for thee*—" I will put my fear into their hearts, that *they* shall not depart from me" (Jer. xxxii. 40). Therefore, *in the covenant* the Bride may truly say, " He shall lie all night betwixt my breasts."

The whole period of the existence of the Church of Christ on earth may be called " the night," for the Resurrection will alone reveal the full light of day. All this time, therefore, the Church would seek to abide in close union and communion with her beloved, Christ *dwelling in her heart* by faith (Eph. iii. 16).

Ver. 14. " *My beloved is unto me as a cluster of camphire in the vineyards of En-gedi.*"

" Camphire," the most highly esteemed, the sweetest and loveliest, and most fragrant of plants in Eastern countries, is the one chosen by the Bride, to express her estimation of her beloved. As " a cluster," too, from the vineyards of En-gedi, where it grew in richest profusion. How it reminds us of what St Paul says, " My God shall supply all your need, according to *his riches* in glory *by Christ Jesus*"*!* (Phil. iv. 19.) We do not half *enjoy*

the sweet fragrance of Jesus as we might. He is
not only " the Lamb slain," to save us from sin, but
" a cluster of camphire," to be unto us as the most
refreshing perfume, the most delicious fragrance.
O that believers did but more *enjoy* Jesus with joy
unspeakable ! not using him only as a bitter herb
for medicine, but as a delicious plant for *actual
enjoyment.*

And if a cluster *from* the vineyard prove so ex-
quisitely sweet, what will it be to *dwell in* the vineyard for eternity ! We may now, by faith, taste the
sweet *foretastes* of heaven's joy, just as the Israelites
did "the cluster of grapes" from the promised land ;
but the land itself is ours, and soon we shall enjoy
the fragrance of Jesus, not "as a cluster" from the
vineyard, but as *the* " *vineyard*" himself!

THE LORD'S ANSWER.

Ver. 15. "*Behold, thou art fair, my love ; behold,
thou art fair ; thou hast doves' eyes.*"

So completely has the Lord covered our vileness
and adorned our nakedness, that he beholds us as
" fair." He has made us such that he can behold us
with delight ! He is not taken up, as we are, with
our *present* state and condition ; past, present, and
future, are one with him. And the little moment
of our existence here, is a mere speck to his eternity.
Therefore he looks not upon us " because we are
black," he does *not* despise us for our present defor-

mities ; but, seeing our brief span of sinful mortality
swallowed up in the ocean of a fathomless eternity,
he regards us *in the everlasting covenant*, as " chosen
in Christ Jesus before the foundation of the world,
to be holy, and without blame before him in love "
(Eph. i. 4, 5) ; and in the fulness of time to be presented " faultless before the presence of his glory
with exceeding joy ; " " *without spot or wrinkle,* or
any such thing " (Jude 24 ; Eph. v. 27). " So
shall the King greatly desire thy beauty " (Ps. xlv.
11). Whatsoever others might think of his Bride,
the Lord looks upon her with holy complacency.
He can discern her comeliness (ver. 5), and the
assurance to the believer is most precious—" Behold,
thou art fair, my love." At this moment, Jesus is
saying so of his Church, of each Christian—" *thou*
art fair ! "

The Bride.

Ver. 16. " *Behold, thou art fair, my beloved, yea
pleasant; also our bed is green.*"

There is something peculiarly sweet in this reply
of the Bride ; there is no vaunting *of herself* upon
the commendation of the Lord, but contrariwise, she
immediately turns to *his* beauty. " Behold, *thou* art
fair, my beloved."

Neither is there anything of false humility, or
denial of her beauty, but only the grateful return of
adoring admiration of him. For, after all, her

beauty was *his*—" Let the beauty of the Lord our
God be *upon us*" (Ps. xc. 17). " The beauty of the
Lord our God ! "

She delighted herself in him—" Thou art fair,
yea, pleasant." Since he has been made unto her
" wisdom" (1 Cor. i. 30), she has learned by experience that his " ways are ways *of pleasantness;*"
and that " at his right hand there are *pleasures* for
evermore" (Prov. iii. 13–17 ; Ps. xvi. 11).

And she owns their *mutual* enjoyment ; " Also,
our bed is green." " He maketh me to lie down in
green pastures," saith David ; or, as it is in the
original, " in pastures of budding grass" (Ps. xxiii.
2). Such being the exquisite *freshness* of delight
and repose enjoyed by the flock of the Good Shepherd in their beloved.

Ver. 17. " *The beams of our house are cedar, and
our rafters of fir.*"

It is scarcely possible to read these words without calling to remembrance the house built by Solomon for the worship and dwelling-place of the Most
High, for which we read that Hiram sent him
" timber of cedar, and timber of fir" (1 Kings vi.
15–18 ; and v. 6–10).

Both are so costly and so desirable, that probably
that may be the main idea suggested. " We know
that if our earthly house (literally, ' *hut* ') of this
tabernacle were dissolved, we have a building of God,
an house not made with hands, *eternal* in the heavens"
(2 Cor. v. 1).

The Temple of Solomon was but the type of the heavenly temple, which is composed of " lively stones" built up upon Jesus, the " living stone," "the chief corner stone, the sure foundation ;" stones so completely taken into himself, that in Rev. xxi. 22, it is written, " The Lord God Almighty and the Lamb *are the temple of it.*"

" Ye also, as lively stones, are built up *a spiritual house*" (1 Pet. ii. 4–7 ; see also Eph. ii. 20, 22 ; 1 Cor. iii. 9 ; Ps. xcii. 13). " Christ, as a Son over his own house, *whose house are we*" (Heb. iii. 6). " The beams of *our* house"—so perfect is their identification—" ye in me, and I in you " (John xiv. 20, and xvii. 21). " In my Father's house are many mansions." Jesus and his Church abide together in the *Father's* house, for we are no more strangers and foreigners, but " of the household of God " (John xiv. 3 ; Eph. ii. 19). " I will dwell in the house of the Lord for ever " (Ps. xxiii. 6 ; lxxxiv. ; xxvii. 4 ; lxv. 4).

There is a striking contrast in this *enduring* building to the " tents" spoken of in ver. 5 ; the perishing abode of the Church on earth, to the " inheritance incorruptible, undefiled, and that fadeth not away, reserved in heaven " (1 Pet. i. 4). " Him that overcometh will I make a pillar in the temple of my God, and he shall go *no more out*" (Rev. iii. 12).

CHAPTER II.

Ver. 1. "*I am the rose of Sharon, and the lily of the valleys.*"

ALL the best commentators ascribe these words to the Bride, and not to Christ; since the original rendering is, "I am a rose of the mere field, and a lily of the mere plain," strongly indicating meanness of extraction. And then the reply of Christ immediately follows—"As the lily among thorns, so is my love among the daughters."

The language is most truly applicable to the Bride, but it is no less truly so of Jesus. He was fragrant as the rose, and fair as the lily. Yet it is written of him, "He shall grow up before him as a tender plant, and as a root out of a *dry ground*" (Isa. liii. 2). Indeed, both flowers are peculiarly emblematical of him. "The rose delights *in shadowy places*, and thence has its name in the original;" whilst the lily thrives in "*the valleys.*"

So the Lord laid aside the glory of his Divine majesty for a season, and, "though he was rich, yet for our sakes became poor," and took on him the

form of a servant" (2 Cor. viii. 9 ; Phil. ii. 8).
For he was "meek and lowly in heart," and had not
where to lay his head! "A root out of a *dry*
ground"—"A rose of the mere field, a lily of the
mere plain." And all this was, that he might set us
an example that we should walk in his steps "with
all lowliness and meekness ;" for "not many mighty,
not many noble are called," but God hath "chosen
the poor *of this world*, rich in faith, and heirs of the
kingdom" (Eph. iv. 2 ; 1 Cor. i. 26 ; James ii. 5).

Yet another thought is suggested by the colour of
these two flowers :—

> " Jesus, the saints' perpetual theme—
> What fragrant odours fill the name
> Of lovely *Sharon's rose !*
> As ointment poured forth, it spreads
> A sweet perfume, an unction sheds,
> Whence joy celestial flows.

> " Meek as *the lily*, too—and *white*,
> The lowly, spotless Nazarite,
> The Lamb for sinners slain !
> With blood bedew'd, his own rich blood,
> For us he pour'd the *crimson* flood ;—
> He died, yet lives again !"

Ver. 2. "*As the lily among thorns, so is my love
among the daughters.*"

What a lovely picture of the Church *in the world!*
"A lily among thorns"—"Sheep in the midst of
wolves"—"Lights in the world" (Matt. x. 16 :
Phil. ii. 15). "We know that *we* are of God, and
the whole world lieth in the wicked one" (1 John
v. 19, Gr.) "So is my love among the daughters."

It is true of each individual—" *the* lily ;" each one is, as it were, singled out by Christ from professors around ; and, oh ! precious truth, *he sees* the " thorns" which surround us, *he knows* the opposition we meet with.

And he places " the lily" in striking contrast to the "thorns." In Hos. xiv. 5, the lily is spoken of in reference to fruitfulness—" He shall grow as the lily," &c. ; teaching us how the fruit-bearing character of the children of God should distinguish them from the waste, barren, fruitless " thorn." This distinctive character, this *manifested* difference, is far too little evidenced by Christians, as separating them from the world around.

But there is yet another thought arising from these words, namely, the electing love of God—" the lily *among* thorns." " I have chosen you *out of* the world" (John xv. 19). " I brought thee *out of* the land of Egypt" (Ps. lxxxi. 10). " Many are called, but *few chosen*" (Matt. xxii. 14). " So is my love *among* the daughters."

The Bride's Reply.

Ver. 3. " *As the apple-tree among the trees of the wood, so is my beloved among the sons.*"

If Christ esteemed his Bride as more excellent than all the daughters, so she esteemed him above all the sons. She compares him to an apple or citron-tree, bringing forth delicious fruit (which

may remind us of " the tree of life that bare twelve
manner of fruits "), so presenting him to view in the
strongest contrast to the sons, whom she compares
to " the trees," literally, " the *wild* trees of the
wood." " Who among the sons of the mighty can
be likened to the Lord ? " (Ps. lxxxix. 6.)   What son
is comparable to " the only begotten of the Father,
full of grace and truth "?

> " *I sat down under his shadow with great delight,*
> *and his fruit was sweet to my taste.*"

" *His shadow.*"   " The *Lord* is *thy shade* upon thy
right hand "—" And there shall be a tabernacle for
a shadow in the day-time from the heat "—" The
shadow of a great rock in a weary land "—" Hide
me under the shadow of thy wings " (Ps. cxxi. 5;
Isa. iv. 6 ; xxxii. 2, and xxv. 4 ; Ps. xvii. 8, &c.)
The wide-spreading and luxuriant foliage of this
apple-tree provides a refuge for the cool refreshment and quiet rest of the Lord's people ; shade
from the heat, and shelter from the storm.   For it
is an abiding shadow.   All other shadows are constantly fleeting, but with the Lord " there is *no*
variableness, neither shadow of turning " (James i. 17).
Therefore we may *dwell* beneath it.   " He that
dwelleth in the secret place of the Most High, shall
abide under the shadow of the Almighty " (Ps.
xci. 1).

Here we may *sit down* in the sweet repose and
quiet rest of faith, even in the midst of conflict.

He hath "made us sit together in heavenly places *in* Christ Jesus" (Eph. ii. 6). And there are seasons when it is especially true, that " their strength is to sit still ;" as Jesus once said to his disciples of old, " Come ye yourselves apart into a desert place, *and rest a while* " (Mark vi. 31). " I sat down under his shadow with great delight."

" *Great delight*."—Religion is no gloomy thing. " In the multitude of my thoughts within me," exclaimed David, " thy comforts *delight* my soul " (Ps. xciv. 19). " The meek shall delight themselves in the abundance of peace." Even now, in our partial enjoyment of heavenly things, we can, " believing, rejoice with *joy unspeakable*." " Let your soul delight itself in fatness "—" Delight thyself in the Lord " (Isa. lv. 2 ; Ps. xxxvii. 4 ; 1 Pet. i. 8 ; Ps. i. 2, &c.)

It were impossible to describe the intense enjoyment and delight experienced by the Lord's people in seasons of such near and close communion, while sitting under his shadow. Nor is this passive enjoyment all that is noticed here ; there is, further, the hand of faith plucking the fruit from the tree. " And his fruit was sweet to my taste."

There is actual feeding upon Christ. " If so be ye have *tasted* that the Lord is gracious "—" Unto you he is precious" (1 Pet. ii. 3, 7). " And of his fulness *have all* we *received* " (John i. 16). " He that *eateth* me, even he shall live by me. For my flesh

is meat indeed, and my blood is drink indeed"
(John vi. 55, 57).

How refreshing is this fruit to the soul that is
hungering and thirsting for God, as the hart
panteth after the water-brooks, or as the dry and
thirsty land where no water is! "His fruit was
sweet to my taste." "How sweet are thy words
unto my taste!" (Ps. cxix. 103 ; Ps. lxiii. 1, &c.)

This is language, alas! that the poor worldling
cannot use ; instead of seeing in Christ this all-
desirable "apple-tree," he sees only "a root out of
a dry ground," without form or comeliness. Instead
of finding his fruit sweet to his taste, he is content
to feed upon "*the husks* which the swine do eat"
(Luke xv. 16).

Ver. 4. "*He brought me to the banqueting-house,
and his banner over me was love.*"

Here the figure is changed from the secret enjoyment of private, holy retirement, to the more public
ordinances — in "the banqueting-house." "They
shall be abundantly satisfied with the fatness of thy
house, and thou shalt make them drink of the river
of thy pleasures!" "A feast of fat things" (Ps.
xxxvi. 8 ; Isa. xxv. 6).

Such is the provision made by the Lord of hosts
for his poor and needy ones. "In my Father's
house," may not each of us say, "there is bread
enough and to spare"? Why, then, do we perish
with hunger?

" Open thy mouth wide, and I will fill it " (Ps. lxxxi. 10). " Whosoever will, let him take the water of life freely " (Rev. xxii. 17). " He brought me to the *banqueting*-house ;" for Christ gives to his Bride, even as Solomon gave to the Queen of Sheba, " all her desire, whatsoever she asked, *beside that* which Solomon gave her *of his royal bounty* " (1 Kings x. 13 ; Eph. iii. 8, 16–21 ; Phil. iv. 19).

It is a royal feast, like that spoken of in Esther i. 3–7, when there was provided " royal wine in abundance, according to the state of the king." And as to " the drinking," the king gave commandment to his officers, " that they should do according to every man's pleasure " (ver. 8). " My God shall supply all your need according to *his riches* in glory !" But there is no carnal rejoicing in Jesus' feast— " The kingdom of God is not meat and drink ; but righteousness, and peace, and joy in the Holy Ghost" (Rom. xiv. 17).

Such a feast Christians peculiarly enjoy in the ordinances of the Lord's house, and, above all, in the Lord's Supper. For then they *meet together* in " the banqueting-house," " for the strengthening and refreshing of their souls," that they may " go from strength to strength," and may " wax stronger and stronger " (Ps. lxxxiv. 7 ; Job xvii. 9) ; this being the gracious purpose of their God concerning them, to lead them on to deeper and yet deeper experience of the rich provisions of his covenant love.

The mention of " the banqueting-house " implies
a season of great rejoicing : " My soul shall be
satisfied as with marrow and fatness, and my mouth
shall praise thee with joyful lips " (Ps. lxiii. 5).
" And in this mountain shall the Lord of hosts make
unto all people a feast of *fat* things, a feast of wines
on the lees, of fat things *full* of marrow, of wines on
the lees well refined. And it shall be said in that
day, Lo, this is our God ; we have waited for
him ; we will *be glad and rejoice* in his salvation "
(Isa. xxv. 6. 9). Often, at such seasons, can the
child of God exclaim with David, " My cup runneth
over " (Ps. xxiii. 5). And if such " unspeakable
joy " be found in the mere foretaste, what shall it
be in heaven, when the transitory communion of
a few saints on earth shall be exchanged for the
whole company of the redeemed of the Lord in glory
for ever and ever ! " Blessed are they which are
called unto *the marriage supper* of the Lamb " (Rev.
xix. 9).

How it will then resound from every tongue, " *He
brought me!*"—*He* redeemed my soul from death—
He led me by the right way—*He* brought me nigh
to God!—" *He* brought me to the banqueting-
house." Yes ; even " *me ;*" He gave himself " *for
me.*" Oh ! how great are the wonders which grace
hath wrought !

But the banner at that feast unfurls the secret—" His
banner over me was love." It was common at
feasts to have the leader's name inscribed upon the

banner ; and the name of *our* great Captain is, " God is love." Love gained the victory ;—the conflict, the triumph, and the glory, were my Beloved's. " He *loved* me, and gave himself for me ; " and if we are conquerors, it is " *through Him* that loved us " (Gal. ii. 20 ; Rom. viii. 37 ; Rev. iii. 21). " Thanks be to God, which giveth us the victory through our Lord Jesus Christ " (1 Cor. xv. 57).

How sweet to repose under such a banner ! " His banner *over* me was love," whilst " *underneath* are the everlasting arms " (Deut. xxxiii. 27).

And each believer may say it was " over *me*," for *I* was rescued by that love from eternal wrath ; *I* am " a prey taken from the mighty," and a trophy of the victory won by my Beloved.

" And we have known and believed the love that God hath to us."

Ver. 5. " *Stay me with flagons, comfort me with apples ; for I am sick of love.*"

Such manifestations of the love of Jesus are well-nigh overpowering to the soul, especially of the young believer. " I am sick of love." The visions that Daniel saw so overcame him, that " straightway there was no strength in him ; " and John, when he saw the Lord Jesus, " fell at his feet *as dead* " (Dan. x. 8–19 ; Rev. i. 12–18 ; see also *Isaiah*, vi. 5 ; *Gideon*, Judges vi. 22 ; and *Paul*, 2 Cor. xii. 7).

Yet the Bride, so far from asking their withdrawment, seeks only to be strengthened for yet further

manifestations—" to be strengthened with might by
his Spirit in the inner man " (Eph. iii. 16). She
would drink yet deeper from the cup of salvation,
and feed yet again on " apples " from that apple-tree
whose fruit was so sweet to her taste. It is like the
earnest breathings of David : " O God, thou art my
God : I have *earnestly* contemplated thee (for so the
words may be rendered) ; my soul *thirsteth* for thee,
my flesh *longeth* after thee," &c. (Ps. lxiii. 1). " Like
as the hart panteth after the water-brooks, so *panteth*
my soul after thee, O God." " Stay me with
flagons, comfort me with apples ; for I am sick of
love." " My soul longeth, yea, *even fainteth*, for the
courts of the Lord " (Ps. lxxxiv. 2). This is a
blessed hungering and thirsting after righteousness,
and the promise (Matt. v. 6) shall not be delayed.

" *In the day* when I cried thou answeredst me,
and strengthenedst me with strength in my soul "
(Ps. cxxxviii. 3) ;—words which were fully realised
in the experience of the Bride, for immediately follows the expression of the supporting presence of
Jesus :—

> Ver. 6. " *His left hand is under my head, and his
> right hand doth embrace me.*"

" He giveth power to the faint, and to them that
have no might he increaseth strength "—" The
Lord upholdeth him with his hand "—" Underneath
are the everlasting arms " (Isa. xl. 29 ; Ps. xxxvii.
24 ; Deut. xxxiii. 27). Such is the security, and

such the blessed, privileged position of the child of
God. The Good Shepherd gathers the lambs (his
feeble ones) in his bosom, *restoring* (Ps. xxiii. 3) and
embracing them. " I will uphold thee with the right
hand of my righteousness" (Isa. xli. 10)—the right
hand of power being here most sweely connected
with love—"and his right hand doth *embrace* me."
" He shall dwell between his shoulders," and so
abide " in safety," because he is " the *beloved* of the
Lord" (Deut. xxxiii. 12). The omnipotence and
almightiness of God become unutterably precious,
when he is known as " the God of love." To be
embraced within that all-powerful hand, from whence
none can pluck us (John x. 28–30), is indeed consolation ; and it is peculiarly realised by the Church
as the Bride of Christ. " His right hand doth *embrace me.*"

The timid believer, too, who, like Peter, is afraid
of the boisterous wind and the stormy sea, may take
comfort from calling to remembrance, that it is this
same powerful hand, constrained by the same love,
that was then, and shall be still, immediately
stretched forth to catch him that is " beginning
to sink " (Matt. xiv. 30, 31). For he is " able to
keep us from falling," and we may safely say with
David in reference to every occurrence, whether in
life or death, " Into *thine* hand I commit my spirit"
(Ps. xxxi. 5).

Such experience denotes a holy tranquillity and
quietude, precisely similar to that described in Isa.

xxvi. 3—"Thou wilt keep him in perfect peace (Heb. 'peace, peace') whose mind is stayed on thee, because he trusteth in thee." There is real reliance on God, and the calm repose of faith. "His left hand is under my head, and his right hand doth embrace me."

It is under similar circumstances that the charge which occurs in the following verse is repeated on two other occasions in this book ; implying that, in the exercise of tender love, the Lord Jesus would fain forbid any hindrance to such exquisite enjoyment on the part of his Bride. The passage is so understood on the authority of many commentators, who render the last words " till *she* please," but the sense is not determined by the original.

> Ver. 7. " *I charge you, O ye daughters of Jerusalem, by the roes, and by the hinds of the field, that ye stir not up, nor awake my love, till* she *please.*"

When we lose such precious and hallowed enjoyment in seasons of communion with the Lord, *the fault is our own—*" Till she please." What a solemn thought !

The reference to " the roes and the hinds of the field," is perhaps best explained by the peculiar characteristics of each, as pointed out in Prov. v. 19 —" The *loving* hind and *pleasant* roe." The selection of pleasing, loving, and tender objects, at once suggests the idea, that, by the dearest and sweetest

delights now experienced by his Bride, the Lord
Jesus solemnly charged the daughters of Jerusalem
not to disturb or break in upon her hallowed communion with himself.   Alas! there will always be
a limit to such seasons, so long as we are militant
here on earth ; there will always be a "*till* she
please."   The Bride either needs to be aroused and
quickened, as in the verses immediately following ;
or to be reminded of her constant call to conflict and
warfare, as in chap. iii. 5–8 ; or to come up from
the wilderness and grow in holy zeal for the welfare
of others, as in chap. viii. 4–12.   She would *indo-
lently rest in her present happiness*, were not the Lord
graciously to rouse her to the sense of her true condition ; and consequently we find him actually dealing thus with her after each repetition of this charge.
Distinct lessons of Christian experience are in each
case brought before us, divinely adapted to different
stages of the Christian life.

THE BRIDE.

Ver. 8. " *The voice of my beloved ! behold, he cometh
leaping upon the mountains, skipping upon the
hills.*"

"The voice of my beloved !"   It is an exclama-
tion of surprise, plainly intimating that that voice
broke in upon a season of silence.   But it was
instantly recognised ; for Jesus was no stranger to
her.   The sheep of Christ's fold " know his voice "

(John x. 4), and gladly welcome it. "Speak, Lord, for thy servant heareth" (1 Sam. iii. 9, 10).

Whatever dulness and deadness may have crept over the Bride, there was none on the part of her beloved. " Behold, he cometh leaping upon the mountains, skipping upon the hills." Like the father of the returning prodigal, " who *ran*," &c. (Luke xv. 20), for his bowels yearned over her.

> " The voice of my beloved sounds
> Over the rocks and rising grounds;
> O'er hills of guilt and seas of grief,
> He leaps, he flies to my relief."—WATTS.

Ver. 9. " *My beloved is like a roe or a young hart; behold, he standeth behind our wall, he looketh forth at the windows, shewing himself through the lattice.*"

So swift is Jesus in drawing nigh to his people, even like a roe or a young hart! He will " make no long tarrying." " Surely I come *quickly!* " (Ps. lxx. 5 ; Rev. xxii. 20). " Behold, he standeth behind our wall "—" a God at hand" (Jer. xxiii. 23). " I stand *at the door* and knock," were the words of Christ to the Laodicean church in her lukewarmness (Rev. iii. 14–20). Sin had raised up *a wall* of separation, which had hid his face ; but " he *standeth behind* the wall."

> " Though often unperceived by sense,
> Faith sees him always near."

Unbelief *hides* Jesus from us, so that, when we sin, though he be standing close beside us, we cannot see

him.   Like Jacob, we may say, " Surely God is in
this place, *and I knew it not*" (Gen. xxviii. 16).   Here
is comfort for the poor, disconsolate believer, who is
walking in darkness and has no light ; the inward
sense of his presence may be lost, but behind the wall
of sin there is Jesus.   He is no further off than "at
the door" of thy heart.   "Behold, he standeth behind our wall."

Nor is this all : " He looketh forth at the windows."
" The eyes of the Lord are over the righteous."   *His
eye* can penetrate that wall through which thou canst
not see.   " He looketh forth." *

Where is the Peter ready to deny his Lord, upon
whom Jesus does not "turn and look " ? (Luke xxii.
61.)   Where is the Nathanael under the fig-tree,
whom Jesus has not *seen?* (John i. 48.)   Where is
the Zacheus-like spirit, " seeking to see Jesus,"
upon whom Jesus has not looked forth ? (Luke xix. 3.
5.)   Or where the returning prodigal whom the
Father does not *see,* "while he is yet a great way
off"? (Luke xv. 20.)   "He looketh forth at the
windows."

" *Shewing himself* through the lattice."   " I will
love him, and will *manifest myself* unto him " (John
xiv. 21).   " And he was known of them in breaking
of bread" (Luke xxiv. 35).   Such are the gracious
manifestations Jesus makes of himself to his Church !
And although " now we see through a glass darkly,"

* " This word 'looketh' is found but three times in Scripture, and
signifieth to look with observation, making diligent search, looking
narrowly."—Rowbotham.

and, as it were, "through the lattice" only, it is still Jesus "*himself*" that we see—"*his own self*."

It is the special office of the Holy Spirit to take of the things of Jesus and "*shew*" them unto us (John xvi. 14, 15). And while "looking unto Jesus," by faith, we get such precious glimpses of "himself," that we cannot but long for his "*appearing*," when we shall "see the King in his beauty," "which in his times he shall *shew*" (Titus ii. 13 ; Isa. xxxiii. 17 ; 1 Tim. vi. 14–16).

Ver. 10. "*My beloved spake, and said unto me, Rise up, my love, my fair one, and come away.*"

Not only "the voice," but *the words* of Jesus are now heard, and they are precious because they are *his*. "He that hath an ear, let him hear what the Spirit saith unto the churches." They are rousing, quickening words. Christ would not have us rest in any frames and feelings, be they happy and comfortable, or disconsolate and bitter. We must be continually "reaching forth unto those things which are before."

"Rise up, my love, my fair one, and come away." "Arise ye, and depart ; for this is not your rest" (Mic. ii. 10). Rest not in any past attainments : rest not at any distance from Jesus ; rest not in ordinances ; rest not in a cast-down and desponding state of mind; "rise up, and come away." Come to the better things which God hath prepared for them that love him.

Christ addresses her in the kindest language—" My love, my fair one ;" and she received his words as spoken *to herself*—" My beloved spake, and said unto *me.*" There is great force in the personal appropriation of the words of Jesus to our own souls. Not a lamb in his fold that is not known to him *by name*, and there is no presumption in appropriating his words to ourselves, no, not even when he says, " My love, my fair one !" His thoughts are " thoughts of peace," and he " *speaks peace* unto his people" (Jer. xxix. 11 ; Ps. lxxxv. 8).

Ver. 11. " *For, lo, the winter is past, the rain is over and gone.*"

What a lovely lesson is taught us here ! The Lord will not dwell upon the wintry state of his Church—neither should we. Whilst he adds figure to figure in subsequent parts of this book, to set forth the loveliness of his Bride, and the blossoming of her graces in the *spring* season, with the ripening of her fruits and flowers in the *summer* and *autumn*, the whole of the winter season is summed up in these few words—" The winter is past, the rain is over and gone." And even these are to tell that it is "*past!*"

" Old things are passed away ; behold, all things are become new "—" You hath he quickened, who were dead," &c. (2 Cor. v. 17 ; Eph. ii. 1, &c.) All the storms of winter have passed away. " I have blotted out, *as a cloud*, thy transgressions, and, *as a thick cloud*, thy sins : return unto me ;" " for, lo, the winter is past, the *rain* is *over* and *gone*." "The iniquity of Israel shall be sought for, and there shall be none ; and the sins of Judah, and they shall not be found" (Isa. xliv. 22 ; Jer. l. 20). Jesus has borne them all away into a land of forgetfulness!

Therefore, dwell no longer in the dust, nor sit in sackcloth and ashes, brooding over past offences ; but learn this lesson from the words of Jesus—when it is winter with thee, follow the example he has left thee in turning away his eyes from thy barrenness : and, looking away from thyself, and all thy wintry coldness, fix thy steady gaze upon the rising beams of " the Sun of Righteousness "—for " he shall be as the light of the morning, when the sun riseth, even a morning without clouds ; as the tender grass springing out of the earth by clear shining *after rain* " (Mal. iv. 2 ; 2 Sam. xxiii. 4).

For so the darkness and gloominess of " winter," the cheerlessness and discomfort of " rain," the gathering clouds and the pelting storms, shall all be dispelled by the quickening rays of the returning sunshine (Eph. v. 8 ; Ps. xlii. 5-8; Ps. cxxvi. 5).

Ver. 12. " *The flowers appear on the earth*."

Here are *evidences* adduced that it is even as the Lord had said. The winter is past, for " the flowers appear on the earth "—" the precious fruits brought forth *by the sun* " (Deut. xxxiii. 14). The budding of " the flowers "—the very first sign of returning spring—is taken notice of ; so the Lord

D

Jesus marks the *first indications* of grace in the soul.
He sees the flower in the bud—the *blossom* as well
as the fruit. " He will not break the bruised reed,
nor quench the smoking flax," nor *despise* "the day
of small things" (Matt. xii. 20 ; Zech. iv. 10).
" *First the blade,* then the ear, and after that the
full corn in the ear" (Mark iv. 28). So graciously
is the first *appearance* of the flowers on the earth
attended to.

> " *The time of the singing of birds is come, and the*
> *voice of the turtle is heard in our land.*"

" The singing of birds " is an acknowledged and
welcome token of the return of spring. And "the
voice of the turtle " (a bird of passage, emphatically
mentioned in Jer. viii. 7, as "observing the time of
its coming ") marks the peculiar season of the year
with double force. Thus we learn that evidences
are not to be lightly esteemed. The spring season,
in the history of St Paul, was noticed by the Lord
in those remarkable words, " Behold, he prayeth."
The low, gentle sound of the turtle's voice is distinctly heard on high, as well as the more cheerful
sound of praise which is heard in the tabernacles of
the righteous.

Ver. 13. " *The fig-tree putteth forth her green figs, and*
the vines with the tender grape give a good smell."

What words of encouragement are here ! " The
tender grape gives a good smell." The youngest

believer—the flower *in the bud*—is fragrant unto
the Lord; and the *yet unripe fruit*—" the *green*
figs "—are acceptable to Jesus! Do we write bitter
things against ourselves because of our unfruitful-
ness? So does not Jesus—" Thus saith the Lord,
I remember thee, the kindness *of thy youth*, the
love of thine espousals," &c. (Jer. ii. 2). The
feeblest attempts of the child of God, the putting
forth of "*green* figs," is noticed and accepted by
Jesus.

"The vines with the tender grape give a good
smell." "The things which were sent from you
(writes St Paul to the Philippians) were an odour
of a sweet smell, a sacrifice acceptable, well pleasing
to God" (Phil. iv. 18). So small a service as the
ministering to the saints, is an odour of a sweet
smell to God. What a comfort this should be to
the saint who is "rich in good works," as an evidence that with him " the winter is past," and the
sun has arisen upon his once frozen heart of stone !
" God is not unrighteous to forget your work and
labour of love" (Heb. vi. 10 ; Rom. vi. 22 ; Hosea
xiv. 8).

" *Arise, my love, my fair one, and come away.*"

> " Rise, my soul, and stretch thy wings,
> Thy better portion trace;
> Rise from transitory things
> Towards heaven—thy native place."

" Awake, awake, put on thy beautiful garments,
O Jerusalem ; shake thyself from the dust ; *arise*

and sit down," &c. (Isa. lii. 1, 2). "*I will arise,
and go to my father.*"

It is a precious invitation, for it is Christ that
calls ; and he does not bid us depart, but "*Come.*"
"Come out, and be ye separate, saith the Lord, and
I will receive you." "Come unto me"—"Come
away" (2 Cor. vi. 17, 18). "Forgetting those
things which are behind, and reaching forth," &c.
(Philip. iii. 13, 14).

> " Rise, saith my Lord, make haste away,
> No mortal joys are worth thy stay.

> " And when we hear our Jesus say,
> Rise up, my love, make haste away,
> Our hearts would fain outfly the wind,
> And leave all earthly things behind."—WATTS.

CHRIST'S INVITATION.

Ver. 14. "*O my dove, that art in the clefts of the
rock, in the secret places of the stairs, let me see
thy countenance, let me hear thy voice ; for sweet
is thy voice, and thy countenance is comely.*"

No figure could more beautifully represent the
Church of Christ, than a dove hid in the clefts of
the rock.

> " Rock of Ages, cleft for me,
> Let me hide myself in thee."—TOPLADY.

" Be thou to me for a rock of habitation, where-
unto I may continually resort"—" In the time of
trouble he shall hide me in his pavilion ; in the
secret of his tabernacle shall he hide me ; he shall

set me upon a rock"—" When my heart is over-
whelmed, lead me to the Rock that is higher than I"
(Ps. lxxi. 3 ; Ps. xxvii. 5 ; Ps. lxi. 2 ; Ps. xxxi. 2. 3).
" The secret places of the stairs" is not a distinct
figure from the rock ; for it has evident reference to
the gardens in the East, where the terraces one above
another were cut *out of* the rock ; and to these terraces the stairs were the ordinary means of ascent.
The timid dove took refuge there, and found it a
secure " hiding-place" and a precious shelter (Isa.
xxxii. 2). " He shall dwell on high ; his place of
defence shall be the munitions of rocks ;" therefore
" trust ye in the Lord for ever ; for in the Lord
Jehovah is the Rock of Ages" (Isaiah xxxiii. 16, and
xxvi. 4, margin).

Thrice blessed they who are hidden in the cleft
of that Rock (Ex. xxxiii. 18–23), that they may see
the goodness of the Lord, and be safe when the
billows swell, and the storm rises high ! It is only
while we are thus " *in* Christ Jesus" that our
countenance beams with the reflection of his glory,
and that his Spirit breathes through us, and makes
our voice *sweet*. But the Father delights in us, *in*
his well-beloved Son, and loves to hear the breathings of " the Spirit of his Son in our hearts, crying.
Abba, Father." " Let me see thy countenance, let
me hear thy voice ; for sweet is thy voice, and thy
countenance is comely." " The prayer of the upright is his delight."

How strange and sad it is that we should be so

silent—so slow to pray, so slow to praise, when Jesus is saying to us, " Let me hear thy voice"! If it is " *sweet*" to him, should we not be offering the sacrifice of praise "*continually*"? (Heb. xiii. 15.) If it be in our power to yield a moment's pleasure to our Beloved, should we not delight to let him hear our voice? Alas! that he should hear our voice so seldom! Our faith in his word is so small, that we barely believe him when he affirms that it is "sweet." Yet he says, "Thy lips, O my spouse, drop as the honeycomb"—"Thy lips are like a thread of scarlet, and thy speech is comely"—" Sweet is thy voice" (Cant. iv. 3, 11). He even loves to hear us speaking *of* him to one another (Mal. iii. 16). And the secret of God's delight in the voice of his people is simply this—" It is not ye that speak, but the Spirit of your Father which speaketh in you" (Matt. x. 20).

For the same reason he sees beauty in their countenance ; for the soul that is much in communion with Jesus reflects *his* beauty, being " changed into the same image, from glory to glory, even as by the Lord the Spirit" (2 Cor. iii. 18). Thus, when Moses was forty days in the mount, " *his face shone*" (Ex. xxxiv. 29), though *he* wist it not. " So shall the King greatly desire thy beauty." " Thy countenance is comely!" " All fair."

THE BRIDE.

Ver. 15. " Take us the foxes, the little foxes, that spoil the vines: for our vines have tender grapes."

The Bride here is all intent upon the care of the vineyard, and conscious of the danger to her " tender grapes " from " the foxes, the little foxes." In Eastern countries, where the gardens and vineyards were cut out of the rocks in terraces, these " little foxes " concealed themselves in great numbers under the luxuriant foliage of the vines, and did great mischief, especially in spring, among the " tender grapes."

Well, therefore, may the Church cry out, " Cleanse thou me from *secret* faults " (Ps. xix. 12) —those subtle and almost unperceived sins which so sadly " spoil the vines." " Let us lay aside every weight, and the sin which doth so easily beset us," " looking *diligently* lest any man fail of the grace of God " (Heb. xii. 1, 15 ; 2 Tim. ii. 16, 17).

" The *cares* of this world, the *deceitfulness* of riches, the lusts and pleasures of life," all which " *choke the word*," so that we become unfruitful, may be understood by these little foxes. They secretly eat away the tender grapes, and spoil the vines ; therefore they should be diligently and earnestly prayed against (Luke viii. 14). This watchful care bespeaks that integrity of heart in the Bride which leads to the precious " assurance "

and " confidence " of faith, expressed in the following verse :—" For if our heart condemn us not,
then have we confidence toward God " (1 John iii.
21). The indulgence of any, the least known sin,
condemns us, and our happy sense of assurance is
clouded ; but in the exercise of strict watchfulness,
it is sweetly realised.

Ver. 16. " *My beloved is mine, and I am his : he
feedeth among the lilies.*"

Here is faith in strong and lively exercise—" the
full assurance of faith," accompanied, as it ever is,
with a *true* heart (Heb. x. 22). " My beloved is
mine, and I am his." It is appropriating faith—a
full realising of her covenant relationship with him.
" My beloved is mine," for he has *given himself* to
me ; " and I am his," for he has *bought me* with his
own blood ! " Ye are not your own, for ye are
bought with a price." Living or dying, we are
" *the Lord's* " (Rom. xiv. 7, 8 ; 1 Cor. vi. 20).

To this the Bride adds, " He feedeth among the
lilies." She has been comparing herself to a vineyard or garden, and now she expresses her belief
that her Beloved is " in the midst of her," feeding
among the plants of his own right-hand planting.

Ver. 17. " *Until the day break, and the shadows
flee away, turn, my beloved, and be thou like a roe
or a young hart upon the mountains of Bether.*"

The " assurance of faith " leads on to the " assurance of hope." For as in verse 16 there was "the full assurance of faith," bringing a sense of *present* peace and enjoyment into the soul, so here there is "the full assurance of hope," *looking forward* to yet fuller and brighter manifestations of her Beloved in his presence, uninterruptedly and for ever. For there, day and night, sunshine and shadow, light and darkness, shall have merged into one eternal day—emphatically called "*the Day*." "Until the day break !"

> "Here often from our eyes
> Clouds hide the light divine !
> There we shall have unclouded skies,
> Our sun will *always* shine."

Even the first rising beams of the Sun of Righteousness, *at the breaking* of *that* day, shall dispel every shadow—"the shadows *flee away*."

Many are the shadows which now hide from our eyes the sight of that glorious day. "For now we see *through a glass* darkly," or "in a riddle" (1 Cor. xiii. 12)—it is but partial light. Ordinances, too, are but the shadow of heavenly things—"a *shadow* of things to come" (Heb. x. 1 ; Col. ii. 16, 17). And our bodies, likewise, screen the light of day from us, for "whilst we are at home in the body, we are absent from the Lord." They hinder our "*sight*" of Jesus, and while in them we can only "walk by faith" (2 Cor. v. 6, 7). But all these shall "flee away." "For when that which is per-fect is come, then that which is in part shall be done away" (1 Cor. xiii. 10). "Thy sun shall no more

go down ; neither shall thy moon withdraw itself :
for the Lord shall be thine everlasting light" (Isa.
lx. 20).   " And there shall be no night there ; and
they need no candle, neither light of the sun ; for the
Lord God giveth them light" (Rev. xxii. 5). " He shall
be as the light of the morning when the sun riseth,
even a morning without clouds" (2 Sam. xxiii. 4).

Such is the believer's prospect for the future ;
and the earnest "looking for that blessed hope"
begets a spirit of prayer in the soul, that " *until* the
day break " we may be " *kept* by the power of God
through faith unto salvation."   " Until the day
break, turn, my beloved ; " or, more literally, " en-
compass "—" be on every side " of me.   Keep me as
in a garrison (1 Pet. i. 5).   Thus, in Ps. lxxi. 21,
the word here rendered " turn," is translated " comfort me *on every side.*"

" And be thou like a roe or a young hart upon
the mountains of Bether" (margin, " division ").
There are yet manifold hindrances and mountains
of separation between us and glory, but Jesus has
broken down every wall of partition.   " And this is
the word of the Lord unto Zerubbabel—Who art
thou, O great mountain ? before Zerubbabel thou
shalt become *a plain*" (Zech. iv. 6, 7).   Often when
we imagine that *mountains* of division lie between us
and Jesus, we find him present with the swiftness of
a roe or a young hart.

Contrast these " mountains of *division* " with the
" mountains of *spices* " in Cant. viii. 14.

CHAPTER III.

THE BRIDE.

Ver. 1. "By night on my bed I sought him whom my soul loveth; I sought him, but I found him not."

WE are almost ready to exclaim—Can such be the language of one who but so lately had said, "A bundle of myrrh is my well-beloved unto me; he shall lie all night betwixt my breasts"? (chap. i. 13.)

It is to be feared, however, that every believing child of God will too well *understand* the sad change by painful experience, to doubt its truth for one moment. And it is experience that frequently follows upon seasons of hallowed communion. There is a liability to *rest* in enjoyment—to cast off the weapons of our warfare, and vainly to indulge the delusive persuasion that all the night season, until the day dawn, may be passed in perfect security and ease. Like David, we are prone in our prosperity to say, "I shall never be moved: Lord, by thy favour thou hast made my mountain to stand strong"

(Ps. xxx. 6, 7). And thus we fall into spiritual darkness, and into a state of carnal ease and slothful indolence, most aptly described as the night season, passed upon a bed of sloth. "By night upon my bed I sought him whom my soul loveth : I sought him, but I found him not."

" Thou didst hide thy face, and I was troubled " (Ps. xxx. 7).

"If thou withdraw, 'tis night."

" Woe to them that are *at ease* in Zion . . . . that lie upon beds of ivory, and stretch themselves upon their couches !" (Amos vi. 1, 4.) It is an unspeakable mercy when the Lord gives the soul no rest in such a state. The promise is, " They shall find me when they search for me with all their heart " (Jer. xxix. 13). No wonder, therefore, that the Bride sought in vain, when she sought him only on her bed. " They have not cried unto me *with their heart*, when they howled upon their beds " (Hos. vii. 14). "There is none that *stirreth up himself* to take hold of thee " (Isa. lxiv. 7). We must not be slothful, but fervent in spirit, if we would walk in communion with Christ (Heb. vi. 12 ; Rom. xii. 11).

Still, although there was indolence, there was yet *sincerity* in the search of the Bride for her Beloved ; " I sought him *whom my soul loveth* " (John xx. 17). And, consequently, there could be no rest or enjoyment in his absence. " With my soul have I desired thee in the night "—" I cry in the night season, and am not silent" (Isa. xxvi. 9 ; Ps. xxii. 2).

How strikingly does such a state altogether contrast with the vigilant watchfulness the Lord requires of his servants when he cometh ! " Blessed are those servants whom the Lord, when he cometh, shall find *watching*. . . . And if he shall come in the second watch, or come in the third watch, and find them *so, blessed* are *those* servants" (Luke xii. 37, 38).

> Ver. 2. " *I will rise now, and go about the city in the streets, and in the broad ways I will seek him whom my soul loveth: I sought him, but I found him not.*"

In this state of restless uneasiness upon her bed, the Bride resolves upon a more diligent search. Like the prodigal, she says, " I will *arise*," &c. And, like him, she not only resolves, but acts. " And he arose," &c. (Luke xv. 18–20). " I sought him," &c. She calls to remembrance the voice of the Good Shepherd (chap. 1. 8), " Go thy way forth *by the footsteps of the flock;* " and at once determines upon seeking him thus in " the city, in the streets, and in the broad ways"—the usual resort of the citizens of Zion. " Not forsaking the assembling of yourselves together" (Heb. x. 25).

" I will *rise* now—I will seek him." Here is real effort, a true evidence of sincerity of purpose. Here is also a restless uneasiness and dissatisfaction with everything short of Christ. " I will seek *him;*" and yet, once more, it is *a present* determination to seek him without delay—" I will rise *now*."

But sensible enjoyment is not immediately re-gained ; "I sought him, but I found him not." Like Job—"O that I knew where I might find him ! Behold, I go forward, but he is not there ; backward, but I cannot perceive him. On the left hand, but I cannot behold him : he hideth himself on the right hand, that I cannot see him" (Job. xxiii. 2, 8, 9). "Now for a season, if need be, ye are in heaviness through manifold temptations," for the "*trial* of your faith" (1 Pet. i. 6, 7). These trying, sifting times work for ultimate good, though the chastening for the present be grievous.

A blessing is often realised in social intercourse ; "That I may be comforted," writes St Paul, "by *the mutual* faith of you and me" (Rom. i. 12) ; of *the "fellow-citizens"* in the household of faith. But it is not always so. We may be in the very midst of means of grace, and yet not find Christ in them, as was the case with the Bride. "I sought him, but I found him not." And now her sincerity was put to a searching test ; would anything *short* of *Christ himself* satisfy ? No. She cannot rest there, for she has not found "*him.*"

> Ver. 3. "*The watchmen that go about the city found me : to whom I said, Saw ye him whom my soul loveth ?*"

"I have set watchmen upon thy walls, O Jeru-salem"—"They watch for your souls as they that must give account " (Isa. lxii. 6 ; Heb. xiii. 17 ; Ezek.

iii. 17 ; Jer. vi. 17). " The priest's lips should keep knowledge, *and they should seek the law* at *his mouth ; for* he is the messenger of the Lord of hosts " (Mal. ii. 7). The Bride was, therefore, making use of those appointed *means* of grace to which God promises his blessing. " I being in the way, the Lord led me " —" The watchmen found me "—a precious token to her that she was indeed in the right way.

She immediately asks them *after Christ,* not even waiting to explain of whom she spake. " Nothing but Christ, nothing but Christ," was ever the language of her heart. Her one question is, " Saw ye *him* whom my soul loveth ? "

There is something of deep interest in *the threefold repetition* of this expression, during the Bride's search after her absent Saviour : " I sought him whom my soul loveth" (ver. 1) ; " I will seek him whom my soul loveth" (ver. 2) ; "Saw ye him whom my soul loveth ? " (ver. 3.) It forms a strikingly beautiful reply to the thrice-repeated question of our Lord to Peter, " Lovest thou me ? " O for that true *sincerity* of love (Phil. i. 10 ; Eph. vi. 24) which may enable us always to answer, " Lord, thou knowest all things ; thou knowest that I love thee "! (John xxi. 15–17.)

But the watchmen were not Christ, and the Bride is not yet satisfied. It is *the Lord's presence in the means,* and not the means themselves, that gives peace and healing. The man lay by the pool of Bethesda " thirty and eight years," but the waters were only *effectual* when an angel stepped in and troubled them (John v. 3–7).

Ver. 4. "*It was but a little that I passed from them, but I found him whom my soul loveth.*"

Precious encouragement! "For in due season we shall reap, if we faint not"—"I said not unto the seed of Jacob, Seek ye me *in vain*"—"Seek, and ye shall find"—"Then shall we know, *if we follow on* to know the Lord" (Gal. vi. 9 ; Isa. xlv. 19 ; Matt. vii. 7 ; Hos. vi. 1–3).

"It was *but a little* that I passed from them ;" she was very near him in the use of the appointed means, still she would not *rest* in the means ; she passed on *from* the watchmen *to* the Lord himself.

It was very like Mary at the sepulchre, seeking for Jesus. The angels "found her," being the divinely appointed guard set to watch the sepulchre ; and when they inquired of her why she wept, she answered, "Because they have taken away *my Lord*," &c. She "passed from them" (for nothing but Christ would do for her), and next addressing herself to one whom she supposed to be the gardener, she earnestly exclaims, "Sir, if thou have borne him hence, tell me where thou hast laid him." She knew not how near Jesus himself was to her all this time—"She knew not that it was Jesus," but, lo! she found him whom her soul loved (John xx. 11–16).

What blessed experience!

"*I held him, and would not let him go, until I had
brought him into my mother's house, and into the
chamber of her that conceived me.*"

"Hold fast that thou hast" (Rev. iii. 11). Like
Jacob wrestling with the angel, say, "*I will not let
thee go,* except thou bless me ;" and, like the disciples, hold fast thy Saviour "by his feet," lest thou
lose him again (Gen. xxxii. 26 ; Matt. xxviii. 9).

"As a little weeping child will hold its mother
fast, not because it is stronger than she, but because
the mother's bowels so constrain her, that she
cannot leave the child ; even so Christ, yearning
over the believer, *cannot go,* because he *will* not."—
DURHAM.

The expression, "my mother's house," seems to
be in allusion to *the second birth of the Spirit* (John
iii. 5–8), by which the soul is brought into vital
union with the Lord Jesus Christ. "That which is
born of the Spirit is spirit." The meaning of the
words, therefore, is, bringing *Christ* into the heart
—"that Christ may *dwell* in your hearts by faith"
(Eph. iii. 17). "My little children," writes the
apostle, "of whom I travail in birth again until
Christ be *formed in you*" (Gal. iv. 19). How wonderful, that our souls should be *the chambers* in
which Jesus dwells !

"I held him, and would not let him go, until I
had brought him into my mother's house," &c.
There is a very powerful meaning in these words, in
the connexion in which they stand. The Bride had

E

lost her own personal communion with Jesus (ver.
1-3), and had to seek him abroad "in the city."
He was, so to speak, absent from "the chamber" of
her heart, and this she could not bear. Truly the
night of life must ever be a restless one, if passed
alone without Jesus!

But this restlessness of the Bride was the proof of
her sincerity. This is exactly *the test* of the true
child of God, as distinguished from the mere profes-
sor. The one is content with a *general* knowledge
of Christ, as present with his Church, &c., but the
other can be satisfied with nothing short of *direct,
personal appropriation* of him—a bringing of him
home to the secret "chambers" of the soul, and a
holy constraining of him to *abide* there! "I held
him, and would not let him go."

CHRIST.

Ver. 5. "*I charge you, O ye daughters of Jerusalem,
by the roes, and by the hinds of the field, that ye
stir not up, nor awake my love, till* she *please.*"

This holy determination to hold fast her Beloved,
is graciously responded to by him, in a repeated
charge to the daughters of Jerusalem that they
should not disturb her (comp. chap. ii. 7). These
are happy seasons, indeed, when for a time the soul
rests by faith in the arms of her Beloved—leaning
on his bosom, in actual realisation of "the communion of the Holy Ghost." Words fail to give utter-

ance to *what* it is, but *St John* seemed peculiarly to
enter into the experience of it, when he said, " Truly,
our fellowship is with the Father, and with his Son
Jesus Christ" (1 John i. 3). This season of repose,
however, is soon exchanged for wilderness journey-
ings. Israel could only rest while the pillar of
cloud and of fire " tarried." Oh ! how sweet it
will be when our journey of love is ended, and we
plunge into the ocean fulness of the God of love
for all eternity !

> Ver. 6. " *Who is this that cometh out of the wilder-
> ness, like pillars of smoke, perfumed with myrrh
> and frankincense, with all powders of the mer-
> chant ?* "

The use of the feminine gender here, in the
original, proves these words to be spoken of the
Bride. " Who is *she* that cometh out of the wilderness ? "

There is evident reference to the wilderness history of the children of Israel, and to the tabernacle
worship, from whence the acceptable incense of
prayer and praise was ever ascending—" incense
of spices" being offered upon the golden altar every
morning, " *for a perpetual incense* before the Lord"
(Ex. xxx. 1–8). For thus every step of the way
was rendered fragrant to the Lord. " Who is she
that cometh out of the wilderness like pillars of
smoke (or smoke of burning incense), perfumed
with myrrh and frankincense, with all powders of

the merchant?" It is a precious thought to believers, that even *now*, in the wilderness of *this* world, they may yield such sweet fragrance to Jesus.

And it has been beautifully remarked, that "some realise much of the wilderness character of this world, and a keen sense of its privations, who but little apprehend it as the place in which they may collect abundance of precious things to enhance their joys hereafter. But associations of trial are not the only ones to be linked with the wilderness; and though, as *natural* persons, we know nothing of 'myrrh and frankincense,' and our privations only elicit murmurings and unbelief; yet, *as renewed in Christ*, they become the very means of developing our Christian graces. And, laden with these fruits, of desert origin, we shall one day, like the Bride, come up out of the wilderness, and remember it only as the place where we gathered the fragrance to be for ever attached to our persons in heaven. Who will complain, then, of the trials and discipline which have been the means of enabling him to obtain these 'powders of the merchant,' and thus to yield to the Lord a perfume unpossessed by any angel above?"

These are precious considerations to such as are (as yet) *but coming out of* "the wilderness." Our " forty years' " wandering there is not in vain. But it is *merely glanced* at here. For this chapter contains within itself a brief and yet comprehensive summary of the Church's history.

In ver. 6, its "*wilderness*" character is referred to.

In ver. 7, 8, it is seen as the Church "*militant here on earth.*"

In ver. 9, 10, Christ is seen dwelling in believers, as the members of his body ; and in ver. 11, there is the final consummation in the kingdom of glory.

> Ver. 7. "*Behold his bed, which is Solomon's ; three-score valiant men are about it, of the valiant of Israel.*"

The word rendered "bed" is properly a "*litter*" or travelling conveyance, still keeping up the idea in the preceding verse of *journeying.* It is the *temporary resting-place* of the King. "Behold his bed, which is Solomon's." The allusion appears to be to the tabernacle, of which it is written, "The ark of God dwelleth within curtains ;" and so God himself speaks of having "walked in a tent, and in a tabernacle," in all the places where he walked with the children of Israel (2 Sam. vii. 2, 6, 7). The ark was the symbol of his presence, and the tabernacle was its "resting-place" (Numb. x. 33–36). Around it the tribes of Israel were encamped throughout their armies, every man by his own standard (Numb. i. and ii.)—as *good* soldiers of Jesus Christ.

Thus the "bed," or resting-place, of King Solomon. stands in most striking contrast to the bed of carnal sloth and ease, spoken of by the Bride in ver. 1— the one, a place of idle security ; the other, of active service.

Ver. 8. " *They all hold swords, being expert in war.*"

" Take the sword of the Spirit, which is the word of God," &c., and fight manfully under the banners of the Captain of your salvation—" For the weapons of our warfare are not carnal, but mighty through God to the pulling down of strongholds " (Eph. vi. 17 ; 2 Cor. x. 4). The Christian life is one of continual warfare ; " there is no casting off weapons." " For we wrestle not against flesh and blood, but against principalities, against powers," &c. (Eph. vi. 12).

We therefore *need* to be " expert," " not ignorant of the devices " of our great enemy (2 Cor. ii. 11). And in order to this, we must *be trained* under our great Leader and Captain : " Blessed be the Lord my strength, *which teacheth* my hands to war, and my fingers to fight " (Ps. cxliv. 1, 2 ; Ps. xviii. 32, &c.) We must be clothed in the " *whole* armour " he has provided for us (Eph. vi. 13, &c.), carefully remembering also, that " no man that warreth entangleth himself with the affairs of this life " (2 Tim. ii. 3, 4). We bear sadly too little of *the soldier's* life and character about with us, though it is the one so especially belonging to us as members of Christ's Church militant here upon earth. The sword should be ever in hand.

> " *Every man hath his sword upon his thigh, because of fear in the night.*"

" Every man "—for it is an individual conflict ;

they *all* hold swords. Not one follower of Jesus but is called to "fight the good fight of faith" (1 Tim. vi. 12 ; 2 Tim. ii. 3).

As it is written of our Captain, " Gird thy sword upon thy thigh, O most mighty," so has the Lord commanded to each of his soldiers, " Put *every man* his sword by his side " (Ps. xlv. 3 ; Ex. xxxii. 26, 27).

Thus, in Neh. iv. 18, we read that " *every one* had his sword girded by his side, and *so* builded." " Your loins girded." It must be an habitual thing, for at the moment of attack no time will be allowed for girding on armour. We must be *ready,* lest it be with us as with the foolish virgins, who, when the cry was made at midnight, " Behold, the bridegroom cometh," had no oil in their lamps !

Let us not have to own, to our shame, that we seek the Lord, if haply we may find him, *by night upon our beds ;* but rather be found " *watching,*" with our loins girded and our lamps burning all through the night of conflict, till the rising " Sun of Righteousness " puts every enemy to flight by his noonday shining (Ps. civ. 22).

Ver. 9. " *King Solomon made himself a chariot of the wood of Lebanon.*"

Another stage of the Church's history is now glanced at. King Solomon no longer abides, as it were, " within curtains ;" but makes for himself a more durable and lasting dwelling-place—"a chariot (margin, 'bed') of the wood of Lebanon." It was emphatically of this wood that the temple was built; it was even called "*an house of cedar*" (2 Sam. vii. 7). "*All was cedar*, there was no stone seen" (1 Kings vi. 15–18). Of this building, spiritually applied, the Lord Jesus is himself the foundation, "the chief corner stone, *in whom* all the building, fitly framed together, groweth unto an holy temple in the Lord" (Eph. ii. 20, 21). We, as lively stones, are built up a spiritual house for the Lord to dwell in. He makes himself a dwelling-place in believers : "*the temple of his body.*"

> Ver. 10. "*He made the pillars thereof of silver, the bottom thereof of gold, the covering of it of purple; the midst thereof being paved with love, for the daughters of Jerusalem.*"

The pillars of "silver" denote durability, and the names of the two pillars, which Solomon set up in the temple of the Lord, signified, "He shall establish," and "In it is strength" (1 Kings vii. 21, margin). "The bottom thereof of gold" bespeaks its amazing costliness. Not only was every part of the house "overlaid with gold," but *even* "*the floor*, within and without" (1 Kings vi. 30) ; and the "purple" denotes royalty.

Such was the royal residence of the true Solomon —the King of kings. It has its spiritual antitype in the Church now, and it shall have its full accomplishment in the heavenly temple, where the faithful ones who have overcome shall be made pillars to go no more out (Rev. iii. 12), the street of the city being "pure gold" (Rev. xxi. 21), and the inhabitants "*kings* and priests," to *reign* as co-kings with Jesus for ever and ever (Rev. xxii. 5).

And yet, its *chief* glory remains to be spoken of —"the midst thereof being *paved with love!*" The very foundation on which it rests is, "*God is love.*" "He that dwelleth in love dwelleth in God, and God in him" (1 John iv. 8, 16).

"He shall *rest* in his *love!*" (Zeph. iii. 17).

Ver. 11. "*Go forth, O ye daughters of Zion, and behold King Solomon with the crown wherewith his mother crowned him in the day of his espousals, and in the day of the gladness of his heart.*"

> "Oh that the months would roll away,
> And bring that coronation day !
> The King of Grace shall fill the throne,
> With all his Father's glories on."—WATTS.

"Behold the bridegroom cometh ; *go ye out* to meet him" (Matt. xxv. 6). "For I have set my King upon my holy hill *of Zion*" (Ps. ii. 6). Therefore, "rejoice greatly, O daughter of Zion ; shout, O daughter of Jerusalem : behold, thy King cometh unto thee !" &c. (Zech. ix. 9).

"*Behold Him.*" For if Sheba's queen came from the uttermost parts of the earth to behold Solomon's glory, how much more should we come forth from our lusts, and from the world, to contemplate His glory who is far "greater than Solomon!" Now the Church reaches the climax of its glorious history. The day of grace is merged into the day of glory. The lowly "Jesus, who was made a little lower than the angels for the suffering of death," is seen "*crowned* with *glory* and *honour*" (Heb. ii. 9). The whole company of the elect being gathered in, *his crown*, which may be said to be composed of sinners saved by grace, is put upon his head, in place of that crown of thorns with which those very sinners "in derision crowned him!"

For this is essentially the crown with which the Holy Spirit (as the author of the new birth in the souls of sinners) may be said to crown him in the day of his espousals. *Then* "he shall see of the *travail* of *his soul*, and shall be satisfied" (Isa. liii. 11); it shall be "the day of *the gladness* of his heart." He shall be anointed with the oil of gladness above his fellows. He shall fully realise "the joy set before him," and shall "come to be glorified in his saints, and to be admired in all them that believe" (Ps. xlv. 7; Heb. xii. 1, 2; 2 Thess. i. 10). For all shall own him as "King of kings and Lord of lords."

> "All hail! the great Immanuel's name!
> Let angels prostrate fall:
> Bring forth the royal diadem,
> And crown him Lord of all.
>
> "Sinners, whose love can ne'er forget
> The wormwood and the gall,
> Come—spread your trophies at his feet,
> And crown him Lord of all.

> " Let every tribe, and every tongue,
>   Around this earthly ball,
> Now shout in universal song,
>   The crowned Lord of all!"

" And on his head were many crowns " (Rev. xix.
12).

CHAPTER IV.

CHRIST.

Ver. 1. " *Behold, thou art fair, my love; behold, thou art fair; thou hast doves' eyes within thy locks.*"

THE Lord is not weary of beholding his Church which he hath purchased with his own blood; nor does he cease to find delight and satisfaction in her.

> " *My* love, through many changes goes ;
> *His* love, no variation knows !"

" Behold, thou art fair, my love "—*still* " fair." But he is not content with the mere general assertion; he deigns to notice the particular graces with which she is adorned —" Thou hast doves' eyes within thy locks." These are *seven* in number (ver. 1–5), emphatically denoting perfection and completeness.

This reference to the dove suggests the thought at once of humility, chastity, harmlessness, and simplicity. It teaches us what delight the Lord takes in the sincerity of his people's affections towards

him. " If thine eye be *single*, thy whole body shall
be full of light" (Matt. vi. 22 ; contrast Matt. v.
28). " *The lust of the eye*" (1 John ii. 16).

> " *Thy hair is as a flock of goats, that appear from
> Mount Gilead.*"

(Margin, " *eat of*" Mount Gilead.) Here the
Church is seen as a flock, grazing on a fruitful
mount. The mention of " a flock" intimates their
multitude, and their feeding together their visible
unity. Their exalted position and privileges are
implied in their feeding on Mount Gilead, which
was renowned for fruitfulness and for its abundant
pasture. " I will feed you in a good pasture."
But we are especially reminded here of the care
that is taken of each individual member of Christ's
flock ; " The hairs of your head are all numbered."
Every lamb in the flock is known and numbered ;
not one shall be found wanting. All shall "appear"
with Christ in glory!

> Ver. 2. " *Thy teeth are like a flock of sheep that are
> even shorn.*"

" Sheep that are even *shorn*"—freed from all
natural encumbrances. " Lay aside every weight,"
&c. (Heb. xii. 1) ; like the blind man, who, when
Jesus called him, "rose, and *casting away his garment*, came to Jesus" (Mark x. 50). " If thine
hand offend thee, *cut it off*;" if ensnared by riches,
" go and sell that thou hast ," and if thou lovest

father or mother more than Jesus, learn of the disciples to give up *all* for him, even as they "straightway left their nets, the ship, *and their father*" (Mark ix. 43–38; Matt. xix. 21, 22; iv. 20, 22). The same idea is conveyed in the figure of the vine (John xv.), all unfruitful branches being cut off, and the fruit-bearing branches being pruned, or "*shorn*."

"*Which came up from the washing.*"

"A flock of sheep, which came up from the washing"—from the fountain open "for sin and for uncleanness"—from "the washing of regeneration and renewing of the Holy Ghost" (Zech. xiii. 1; Titus iii. 5). "For ye are washed, for ye are sanctified, for ye are justified, in the name of the Lord Jesus and by the Spirit of our God" (1 Cor. vi. 11).

"These are they which came out of great tribulation, and have washed their robes, and made them white in the blood of the Lamb" (Rev. vii. 14; Isa. i. 18; Rev. i. 5, 6).

"A flock of sheep, which came up from the washing." There could not be a more beautiful representation of the purity of that Church for which the Good Shepherd laid down his life, "that he might sanctify and cleanse it with the washing of water by the word; that he might present it to himself a glorious church, not having spot, or wrinkle, or any such thing; but that it should be holy and without blemish" (Eph. v. 26, 27). All defilement cleansed and washed away!

" *Whereof every one bear twins, and none is barren among them.*"

" Such a flock of sheep would greatly enrich their owner."—DURHAM.

Are we not hence taught " what is the riches of the glory of *his* inheritance *in the saints*"? (Eph. i. 18, 19). The Lord chooses to enrich himself through the abounding fruitfulness of his people ; " being filled with the fruits of righteousness, which are by Jesus Christ to the glory and praise *of God.*" " Herein is my Father glorified, that *ye* bear much fruit" (Phil. i. 11 ; John xv. 8 ; Eph. ii. 10 ; 1 Cor. xv. 58). Therefore we are exhorted to give all diligence to add to our faith virtue, &c. &c., that we may " *neither be barren nor unfruitful* in the knowledge of our Lord Jesus Christ" (2 Pet. i. 5–8).

There may probably be especial reference to the conversion of our fellow-sinners here intended ; that every one who has tasted for themselves that the Lord is gracious, should labour to bring others also into the fold, and " turn many to righteousness."

" Then will I tell to sinners round,
What a dear Saviour I have found."

The Hebrew word translated " barren," signifies that none of them is *bereaved or robbed of its young,* denoting the steadfastness of each member of the

Church of Christ. Not one is lost—not one wanting. " None is barren among them."

Ver. 3. " *Thy lips are like a thread of scarlet, and thy speech is comely.*"

The one all-absorbing theme with the lambs of Christ's flock is redeeming love ; their words being all, as it were, dyed in the blood of the Lamb of God—their lips " like a thread of scarlet." It was the subject of prophecy from the beginning (see Gen. iii. 15 ; Ps. xxii. ; Isa. liii. ; Zech. xiii. 7).

It was the one grand object set forth in the types and sacrifices of the law (Gen. xxii ; compare Leviticus with Hebrews). And as it is *now* the one subject under the gospel for preaching, &c. (" We preach Christ crucified," &c.—1 Cor. i. 23, &c. ; 1 Cor. ii. 2 ; Gal. vi. 14), so shall it be throughout eternity the song of the redeemed in glory — " Worthy is the Lamb that was slain," and has redeemed us to God by his blood, &c. (Rev. v. 9, 12).

Let us then see that ours be blood-dyed speech, that so it may be " comely" in the ears of Jesus. No language can be more comely in our lips than that of deep self-abasement. " God be merciful to me a sinner." How often we have need to cry, " Let the words of my mouth, and the meditation of my heart be acceptable in thy sight, O Lord, my strength *and my Redeemer* "*!* (Ps. xix. 14.)

" *Thy temples are like a piece of a pomegranate within thy locks.*"

The pomegranate is a sweet, delicious fruit ; the temples are the seat of *thought*. The idea, therefore, seems to be exactly that described by the Psalmist, " My meditation of him shall be sweet"— " My soul shall be satisfied as with marrow and fatness, when I remember thee upon my bed, and meditate on thee in the night watches" (Ps. civ. 34 ; Ps. lxiii. 5, 6).

There is also implied a true modesty and " shame-facedness" in the term " within thy locks." There is no display—no uncovering of the head (1 Cor. xi. 5), but the reverse. And this *inward* adorning, " the ornament of a meek and quiet spirit," is of great price in the eyes of Him with whom we have to do.

Ver. 4. " *Thy neck is like the tower of David, builded for an armoury, whereon there hang a thousand bucklers, all shields of mighty men.*"

David was emphatically " a man of war." It was his to bring the whole land into subjection for his son Solomon ; and it appears that, in memory of his achievements, he built an armoury whereon were hung the trophies of his mighty men of valour. We read in 2 Kings xi. 10, that " King David's spears and shields were in the temple of the Lord." Does not this teach us, that the Christian's armour is being " strong *in the Lord*"? " For this

F

is the victory that overcometh the world, even our *faith*"—faith being elsewhere described as *the shield* wherewith we " quench all the fiery darts of the wicked" (Eph. vi. 10, 16 ; 1 John v. 4).

And just as each shield and buckler preserved in that armoury added to the fame and renown of King David, so shall every soul won to Jesus, as fresh spoil from the enemy's camp, redound to *His* glory, when, " in the ages to come," each believer shall be displayed to the astonished gaze of princi-palities and powers, *hung upon him* (as upon " a nail in a sure place," Isa. xxii. 23, 24), a trophy of *his* victory over sin and Satan !

When a stronger than the strong man armed comes upon him and overcomes him, *he takes from him all his armour*, wherein he trusted, and that very armour becomes a witness to the might of the great Captain of our salvation.

All, all redounds to the glory of that Victor, through whom " we are more than conquerors " (Rom. viii. 37).

> Ver. 5. " *Thy two breasts are like two young roes that are twins, which feed among the lilies.*"

" Two young roes that are *twins*," seems to imply the idea of *unity* in the Church of Christ—all being " perfectly joined together in the same mind and in the same judgment, that there be no divisions " (1 Cor. i. 10) ; and none of the spirit of Diotrephes, " who loveth to have the pre-eminence " (3 John 9).

" In honour preferring one another "—" Yea, all of
you be subject one to another ;" and, " be kindly
affectioned one to another with *brotherly* love "—as
twins — " endeavouring to keep the unity of the
Spirit in the bond of peace " (Rom. xii. 10 ; 1 Pet.
v. 5 ; Eph. iv. 3).

And there is something beyond this in their
feeding among the lilies—it expresses communion.
For when Jesus is said (chap. ii. 16) to feed among
the lilies, it is evidently in allusion to the communion he enjoyed with the sheep of his pasture ; and
so here it is that the flock enjoy communion " with
each other and the Lord." They all eat the same
spiritual meat, and drink the same spiritual drink,
going to the house of God in company, feeding in
the same " green pastures," and finding therein
mutual refreshment and growth in grace. " Desire
the sincere milk of the word, that ye may grow
thereby " (1 Cor. x. 3, 4 ; Ps. xxiii. 2 ; 1 Pet. ii. 2).

Ver. 6. " *Until the day break, and the shadows flee
away, I will get me to the mountain of myrrh,
and to the hill of frankincense.*"

Exactly what the Bride had prayed for (chap. ii.
17), Jesus here promises to her. So perfectly in
harmony are the breathings of the same Spirit, in
Christ and in his people ! " *I will* get me to the
mountain of myrrh, and to the hill of frankincense,"
and there will I tarry, even " until the day break,
and the shadows flee away ! " " Lo, I am with you

alway, even unto the end of the world." "I will
never, never leave thee, never, never forsake thee"
—for such is the force of these words in the original
(Heb. xiii. 5 ; Matt. xxviii. 20). "This is the hill
which God desireth to dwell in ; yea, the Lord will
dwell in it for ever" (Ps. lxviii. 16).

Ver. 7. " *Thou art all fair, my love ; there is no spot
in thee.*"

Not content with the fourfold repetition of the
fairness of his Bride (in chap. i. 15, and iv. 1), the
Lord adds yet further, "Thou art *all* fair, my love;
there is *no spot* in thee!" " All fair ;" *for* the
beauty of the Lord our God is upon us (Psalm xc.
17). No wonder our beauty is perfect through *his*
comeliness *put upon us* (Ezek. xvi. 14). Our God
no longer beholds us as clothed in our own "filthy
rags," but in the Son of his love. For we are no
longer twain, but one flesh. "As he is, so are we!"
—"all fair."

And thus graciously does the Beloved of our
hearts regard us. He chides us not for our shortcomings and manifold imperfections ; but wraps us
up, as it were, in his robe of righteousness, and then
rests in his love, and joys over us with singing
(Zeph. iii. 17).

Truly, "blessed is the man unto whom the Lord
will not impute sin." "There is no spot in thee."

No spot in *me!* exclaims the astonished believer ;
and yet Job could say, "Behold, I am *vile*;" and

Isaiah could say, " Woe is me, for I am . . . a man
of *unclean lips!*" and Paul could say, " In me, that
is in my flesh, dwelleth no good thing—O *wretched
man* that I am !" and David could say, " I acknowledge my transgressions, and *my sin* is ever before
me" (Job xl. 4 ; Is. vi. 5 ; Rom. vii. ; Ps. li.) And
even the Bride herself could say, " I am *black!*"

Peter, too, could thrice deny his Lord ; and James
and John could desire to call down fire from heaven ;
and of *all* his disciples Jesus could say, " O faithless
and perverse generation." And of the Churches of
Ephesus, Pergamos, and Thyatira he could say, " But
I have a few things *against thee;*" and of Sardis, " I
have not found thy works perfect before God ;" and
of Laodicea, " Because thou art lukewarm, and
neither cold nor hot, I will spue thee out of my
mouth" (Rev. ii. and iii.)

Are we, then, better than they ? No, in nowise.
For is it *of our own* holiness Jesus speaks, when he
says, " There is no spot in thee " ? God forbid ! He
speaks of *his own* comeliness, which he puts upon us,
and *in which* he is able to present us "*faultless* before
the presence of his glory"—before that *excess of
brightness* in which he dwells—" holy and unblameable, and unreprovable in his sight" (Jude 24 ;
Col. i. 22). " Complete in him " (Col. ii. 10). " A
glorious church, *not having spot,* or wrinkle, or any
such thing ; but holy and *without blemish*" (Eph. v.
27).

Alas ! there are few believers who are ready at

once to acknowledge their *perfect spotlessness*—but few who are able to see themselves once and for ever " perfect in Christ Jesus !" And yet, if it be *His* righteousness in which they stand, how can there be a spot in it ? and which of them expects to stand in the judgment, clad in any other ? Then, though they be the vilest of sinners in their own sight, if only they are united to Jesus by simple faith, there is " no spot" in them. There cannot be. Christ can have no diseased member in his body. He is the Great High Priest, whose body-covering robe extends from the head to the feet, without a seam, entirely hiding from view every trembling sinner whose faith has touched but the hem of his garment. Let us learn to hide deeper in Jesus, " hating even the garment spotted by the flesh," touching no un- clean thing, and keeping ourselves " unspotted from the world " (Jude 23 ; 2 Cor. vi. 17 ; James i. 27). " *All fair—no spot !*"

> Ver. 8. " *Come with me from Lebanon, my spouse, with me from Lebanon: look from the top of Amana, from the top of Shenir and Hermon, from the lions' dens, from the mountains of the leo- pards.*"

" By these mountains here, we conceive, are under- stood, the most excellent, choice, and eminent satis- factions of earth, wherein men of the world delight : therefore the Bride is called to leave them to the men of the world, whose property they are, even as

mountains are the abode and delight of wild beasts."
—Durham.

Lebanon was renowned for its beauty and surpass-
ing excellence, though, from Hab. ii. 17, it seems
also to have been the abode of wild beasts; and
"Shenir and Hermon" were the tops of two hills
(mentioned in Deut. iii. 9; 1 Chron. v. 23; Ps.
xxix. 6, &c.) Hence the force of the figure appears
to be, that beneath the highest elevations of earthly
exaltation there lie concealed and hidden dangers
ready to break forth, from whence the Lord, in
tender love, calls his Bride away. " Come with me
from Lebanon, &c.; from the lions' dens, and from
the mountains of the leopards." The roaring lion,
who walketh about, seeking whom he may devour,
wilily makes earth's most attractive regions the seat
of his den. Christ, therefore, calls his Bride to bid
adieu to that scene of danger, and, looking over the
tops of all created excellencies, to set her affection
on things above, and not on things *on the earth*—not
lingering to look *back* on the enjoyments of the world,
but pressing on to the things which are before; to
look " from " them.

> "He calls me from the lions' den,
> From this wild world of beasts and men,
> To Zion, where His glories are;—
> Not Lebanon is half so fair—
>
> "Nor dens of prey—nor flowery plains—
> Nor earthly joys—nor earthly pains—
> Shall hold my feet, or force my stay,
> When Christ invites my soul away."—Watts.

And the invitation is most sweet—" *with me.*"

"Come with me from Lebanon, my spouse, *with me* from Lebanon."   "I long to be *with Jesus!*"

> Ver. 9.   "*Thou hast ravished my heart, my sister, my spouse; thou hast ravished my heart with one of thine eyes, with one chain of thy neck.*"

(Margin, "taken away.")   What marvellous words are these!   Christ "ravished" by his Church !   His heart "taken away."   It is a word nowhere else used in Scripture ; but truly this is a most wondrous chapter.   To see the Lord so ravished with his Bride's beauty, and to hear such gracious words proceed out of his mouth, does indeed unfold to us somewhat of the *satisfaction* of the Lord Jesus when he sees of the travail of his soul.   His heart is ravished—taken away !

And why do we refuse to be comforted by such precious truths ?   It is not *pride* to believe what he says—it is not self-exaltation : it is only glorying *in the Lord*.   And who would not glory in being espoused to *such* a husband ? in having *such* a brother ?   For he calls us his "*sister*," his "*spouse!*" And it is because of this union that he rejoices over us ; for the husband and wife being no longer twain, but one flesh, he sees us *in himself* and *as a part* of himself !   "As the bridegroom rejoiceth over the bride, so shall thy God rejoice over thee" (Isa. lxii. 5).

This is the "great mystery" of this book—Christ and his disciples are *one*.   And it is our actual pri-

vilege to share his joy—" These things have I spoken
unto you that *my joy* might remain *in you*, and that
your joy might be full " (John xv. 11).

But this is not all the wonder of this verse ; it is
not merely that Christ is ravished by his Church
collectively, but, he says, " Thou hast ravished my
heart with *one* of thine eyes, with *one* chain of thy
neck !" With *each* member individually ! " I dwell
in the high and holy place, with *him* also that is of a
contrite and humble spirit,' &c.—" Joy shall be in
heaven over *one* sinner that repenteth "—" It was
meet that we should make merry and be glad, for
this my *son* was dead and is alive again ; *he* was lost
and is found " (Isa. lvii. 15 ; Luke xv. 7, 24, 32).
Yes, *each* returning prodigal gives joy and delight to
Jesus. Each *one* who fears the Lord and thinks
upon his name, shall be a jewel throughout eternity,
to reflect the brilliancy of the Sun of Righteousness.
" Thou hast ravished my heart with *one* of thine
eyes, with *one* chain of thy neck ! "—If *one* sheep be
lost, the good shepherd will " go after " it until he
find it—if *one* piece of silver be missing, the woman
will sweep her house, with a lighted candle, till it is
found !

Rowbotham explains it thus :—" In that he saith,
with *one* eye, and *one* chain, observe, that where
Christ seeth the least grace, he is much taken with
it. It is as if he had said, ' Though I see but one
of thine eyes, to wit, one single look of faith—or
one chain, to wit, one spiritual discovery of myself,

it is enough for ever to take up my heart and affections.'"

> Ver. 10. *" How fair is thy love, my sister, my spouse! how much better is thy love than wine! and the smell of thine ointments than all spices!"*

This is *Christ's* estimate of the love of his Church. No matter, then, if the lowly believer be lightly esteemed in the eyes of an ungodly world—" He seeth not as man seeth." His own love is reflected in the love of his Church, therefore it is " fair," and " better than wine." We know how the Lord Jesus esteemed the love of the poor woman (whose *many* sins being forgiven, made her " love much ") far above all the good things provided at the feast of Simon the Pharisee! (Luke vii. 36–50.) And thus he esteems also the love of his attached, though suffering, members on earth, far above the works of his creation; even as the father of a beloved family takes more delight in his children than in all his possessions.

It is his own love reflected back upon himself; therefore, as his was, so is hers—" much better than wine." (Compare chap. i. 2, 4.) It was *a sister's love*, for " he is not ashamed to call us brethren;" and it was *a wife's love*, for he calls himself our " husband " (Isa. liv. 5). " Whosoever shall do the will of God. the same is my brother, and my sister, and mother " (Mark iii. 35).

The smell of her ointments, too, was sweeter than

all spices ; for it was the fragrance arising from the fruits of his own Spirit implanted in her.

The secret of all the Lord's delight in his Church is this, that it is *his own* work in us—" We love him because he first loved us." So then " boasting is excluded," for it is all of grace. " *Christ* is all and in all."

Ver. 11. " *Thy lips, O my spouse, drop as the honeycomb ; honey and milk are under thy tongue.*"

" The honeycomb *drops actually* but sometimes ; but it always hangs full of honey—sweet drops ready to fall."—SCOTT.

So " out of the abundance of the heart, the mouth speaketh "—" My doctrine shall drop as the rain " (Matt. xii. 34 ; Deut. xxxii. 2). The contrast is very striking between " the multitude of words" spoken of in Prov. x. 19, and speech *dropping* only as the honeycomb. " He that refraineth his lips is wise "—" A word spoken in due season, how good is it !" (Prov. xv. 23.)

But ere there can be the dropping of the honeycomb from our lips, there must have beeen the diligent *gathering in* of *the honey* from flower to flower. And this must be done by feeding on the Word of God for ourselves—*hiding* it in our hearts—*eating* it (Ps. cxix. 11 ; Jer. xv. 16). Our treasures must first be laid up in heaven, and then our hearts and our *conversation* will be there (Matt. vi. 20, 21 ; Phil. iii. 20). So shall we " be ready always to give an answer," &c. (1 Pet. iii. 15, 16).

This is very beautifully represented in the figure of "honey and milk" being under the tongue. For "milk and honey" were among the chief characteristics of the fruitfulness of the land of Canaan; and the Church of Christ ought to be always in the same well-stored condition—her lips dropping as the honeycomb, full of sweet drops ready to fall whensoever a due season offers; and under her tongue "honey and milk," words of kindness and tenderness, like the "gracious words" which proceeded from Jesus' lips (Luke iv. 22; contrast Ps. lv. 21).

> "*And the smell of thy garments is like the smell of Lebanon.*"

Our very "*garments*" should also testify of us that we have been with Jesus—"All *thy* garments smell of myrrh, and aloes, and cassia," &c. (Ps. xlv. 8); so *ours* should retain the scent of Lebanon—"His branches shall spread, and his smell be as Lebanon" (Hos. xiv. 5–7).

It is like the precious ointment that ran down to *the skirts of his garments* (Ps. cxxxiii. 2). Oh! how we ought to hate "even the garment spotted by the flesh"! (Jude 23.)

> Ver. 12. "*A garden enclosed is my sister, my spouse; a spring shut up, a fountain sealed.*"

The main idea suggested by these words is that of the Church being God's own peculiar property; "know that the Lord hath *set apart* him that is

godly *for himself*" (Ps. iv. 3). He hath reclaimed
for himself, from the barren, uncultivated, " waste
howling wilderness," *a* " *garden*," a little, choice,
fruitful, well-cared-for spot. And he hath marked
it as his own special property, for it is " enclosed ;"
he hath " *fenced it*" (margin, " made a wall about
it"), and planted a hedge around it. (See Isa v. 1,
&c.)

He is himself " the husbandman" (John xv. 1) ;
the plants are all the " trees of righteousness" of his
own right hand planting ; and the Lord Jesus is
" *the dresser* of the vineyard." He calls it his own
garden in chapter v. 1. " I am come into *my* garden, my sister, my spouse." It is a little spot
" chosen *out of* the world," reclaimed by sovereign
grace, and *encompassed by* Jehovah, even " as the
mountains are round about Jerusalem" (Psalm cxxv.
2). " For I, saith the Lord, will be unto her a wall
of fire round about, and will be the glory in the
midst of her" (Zech. ii. 5). Contrast Psalm lxxx.
9–13 ; the fence broken down !

" A spring *shut up*, a fountain *sealed*." It was the
custom in Eastern countries, for the royal well to
have the king's seal affixed to it ; others could have
no access to it. It is thus that we are " sealed unto
the day of redemption"—for " the foundation of
God standeth sure, having this seal, The Lord
knoweth them that are his" (Eph. iv. 30 ; 2 Tim.
ii. 19). Thus he says of his Church, " I the Lord
do keep it ; I will water it every moment : lest any

hurt it, I will keep it night and day" (Isa. xxvii. 3). I will set my seal upon it—it is *mine*.

" Thou shalt be like a watered garden, and like a *spring* of water, whose waters fail not" (Isa. lviii. 11; Numb. xxiv. 5, 6). " A well of water springing up into everlasting life" (John iv. 13, 14). How different the " spring" which has " the Fountain of living waters" for its source, from the streams which flow only from the *creature!* These are described by Job as the streams which " pass away," " go to nothing, and perish" (Job vi. 15–18). That which is of man perishes ; while that which is of God en- dures unto eternal life. The Good Shepherd leads his flock " beside the still waters," in his own enclosed garden.

Ver. 13. " *Thy plants are an orchard of pomegra- nates, with pleasant fruits.*"

Christ now compares his Church to " an orchard." For it is not *only* a garden, filled with lovely flowers, but " an orchard," filled with choice *fruit trees.* Every plant in that garden is expected to bring forth " fruit." " He looked that it should bring forth grapes" (Isa. v. 2). For " herein is my Father glo- rified, that ye bear much fruit ; *so* shall ye be my disciples"—" Filled with the fruits of righteousness, which are by Jesus Christ, unto the glory and praise of God" (John xv. 8 ; Phil. i. 11).

They are " *pleasant* fruits," because they are the fruits of the Spirit—and " for *his pleasure* they are and were created ;" " the planting of the Lord, that *he* might be *glorified.*"

Alas! that there should ever be barren fig-trees found in the Lord's garden, branches in Christ that do not bear fruit! (John xv. 2) ; " Every branch that beareth not fruit in me."—ROMAINE. But what a precious truth, that Jesus will intercede for trees that have stood barren for " *three years!*" and will purge and prune them, " that they may bring forth more fruit!" Sooner or later, the Lord's people *will become* fruit-bearing branches ; for each one is " an orchard," and in each one " pomegranates with pleasant fruits" must be found.

Nor is it one kind of fruit only, but many ; " pomegranates *with* pleasant fruits," namely—

> Ver. 13, 14. " *Camphire, with spikenard; spikenard and saffron ; calamus and cinnamon, with all trees of frankincense; myrrh and aloes, with all the chief spices.*"

See what the Lord finds, *and expects to find,* in his Church! What diversity of plants! and what choice fruits! The fruits of the Spirit are manifold —" love, joy, peace, long-suffering, gentleness, goodness," &c. (Gal. v. 22, 23).

The Lord looks for *all* these in his Church, and in each member of it. He would have us abound in " every grace." " As ye abound in every thing, in faith, and utterance, and knowledge," &c., " see that ye abound in *this* grace also" (2 Cor. viii. 7).

If but one be wanting, the Lord takes notice of it. For " God is able to make *all* grace abound toward you ; that ye, always having *all-sufficiency* in *all* things, may abound to *every* good work " (2 Cor. ix. 8–10). There is grace to enable us to abound in *all;* wherefore, then, are we so stunted, so meagre, so sparing? " Ye are straitened in your own bowels," says the apostle. " Ye have not, *because ye ask not.*" See how St Paul prayed for his Colossian converts— " That ye might walk worthy of the Lord unto *all* pleasing, being fruitful in *every* good work : strengthened with *all* might . . . unto *all* patience and long-suffering with joyfulness" (Col. i. 9–11).

> " Thou art coming to a King ;
> *Large* petitions with thee bring ;
> For his grace and power are such,
> None can ever ask too much."

Should we not learn hence to make larger demands upon God's treasury of grace, lest, when he comes to reckon with us, he should find his talents laid by in a napkin, and hid in the earth ; and lest the seed which he has sown in our hearts should lie dormant there, and no " pleasant *fruits* " have been borne by us?

Oh! to " bring forth *more* fruit!"—" fruit *a hundredfold*"—" fruit unto holiness " ! (Rom. vi. 22.)

But these " pleasant fruits " may be regarded in another point of view. The Lord, in looking down upon his garden, and inspecting his vineyard, does not expect all his plants to be alike. In one he sees a pomegranate ; in another, camphire ; in another, spikenard, &c. And these several plants are of totally different characters. Thus frankincense, myrrh, and aloes, are said to grow very *tall*, while spikenard and saffron only just grow above the ground. So, amongst believers, there are "differences of administration, diversities of operations." One is suited for one place in the vineyard, another for another place; but the Lord owns and accepts each; they are *all* his "pleasant fruits;" for it is the same God which worketh all in all (1 Cor. xii. 4–6).

Ver. 15. "*A fountain of gardens, a well of living waters, and streams from Lebanon.*"

This verse has been differently rendered by commentators; some making it applicable to the Church, and others to the Lord himself. Thus, Fry renders it, "The fountain of thy gardens is a well of living waters, and streams flowing from Lebanon." If this be correct, we have the words of Christ to teach us, that "the well of living waters" is the Holy Spirit, flowing from himself, for the quickening and refreshing of his garden—the Church. "The water that I shall give shall be in him a well of water, springing up into everlasting life." "He that believeth on me, out of his belly shall flow rivers of living water. (But this spake he *of the Spirit*, which they that believe on him should receive)" (John iv. 13, 14, and vii. 38, 39). For *He* is the Source, the secret spring of life—the

conductor of the streams of living water, from the
Fountain of living waters, into the garden of Christ.
" It is the Spirit that quickeneth."   A garden that
lacks moisture is soon dried up and languishing.
Its fruitfulness is vitally connected with its being
well watered (see Amos iv. 7).   And, therefore, in
the garden which the Lord God planted, "a river
went out of Eden, *to water* the garden" (Gen. ii.
8, 10).   Hence, also, we find the Psalmist describing
his soul as *thirsting* after God, like "a dry and
thirsty land where no water is" (Ps. lxiii. 1 ; see also
Ps. xlii. 1).   But the fountain of *this* garden "is
a well of living waters, and streams from Lebanon"
—at once *springing up* out of the believing soul,
and *flowing down* from above, as it were from the
heights of Lebanon (James i. 17).

Thus it seems most in accordance with the spirit
of the passage, to take these words, like the rest,
as spoken by Christ to his Bride.   She is "*a garden
inclosed, a spring shut up, a fountain sealed*," and
"an *orchard*" of pleasant fruit trees : but she is all
this of herself, independently of what she is *to
others*.   It is therefore added, that she is "a
fountain of gardens, a well of living waters, and
streams from Lebanon ;" for it is in watering others
that she is herself to be watered (Prov. xi. 25).
In direct opposition to the fountain spoken of by
Jeremiah (chap. vi. 7, " as a fountain casteth out
her waters, so she casteth out her wickedness"),
she is to be a fountain, reflecting the image of "the

Fountain of Living Waters"—a means of life to others. She is to be *a well* of living water; not a shallow stream, but filled with the Spirit of life, whose work does not rest on the surface, but penetrates into the innermost depths and recesses of the soul—a *standing well*, and not a little rivulet that may often be found dried up. And she is yet further to be as "streams from Lebanon," ever flowing forth to water all around, comforting others with the comfort wherewith she has been comforted of God; and gushing forth in clear and invigorating streams, received fresh from the heights of heaven, to quicken and reanimate such as are slumbering and faint.

Oh! to drink deeply and freely of the fountain of the water of life!—with joy to draw water from the wells of salvation! (Rev. xxi. 6 ; Isa. xii. 3.)

> " Dear Fountain of delight unknown !
> Giver of life and joy supreme !
> Ever o'erflow, and pour me down
> A living and life-giving stream."—COWPER.

Ver. 16. *" Awake, O north wind; and come, thou south ; blow upon my garden, that the spices thereof may flow out."*

The Lord Jesus has now surveyed with delight his garden—his spiritual Eden. He has inspected his orchard, and noticed his lovely plants and pleasant fruits. He has examined them *particularly* —not one is overlooked. He found them very choice—" *chief* spices," &c. But yet they do not yield him all the fragrance they might. There seems to be a stillness pervading the garden, so that the spices thereof do not "*flow out*." He, therefore, calls for the fresh outpouring of his Spirit upon it—"*Awake*, O north wind; and come, thou south; *blow* upon my garden." "The wind bloweth where it listeth," &c., "so is every one that is born *of the Spirit.*" The words, spirit, breath, life, and wind, are all used in Scripture in reference to the Holy Ghost; for " it is the Spirit that quickeneth" (John vi. 63). " Come from the four winds, O *breath*, and breathe upon these slain, that they may live" (Ezek. xxxvii. 9). "Awake, O *north* wind," with thy piercing blasts, arousing, quickening, and convincing of sin; "and come, thou *south*," with thy gentle, soothing influences, to breathe comfort, and peace, and heavenly consolations into the soul.

Thus the Lord, in omniscient love, *adapts* these different experiences to the requirements of the various plants. At the right moment, he bids the north wind "*awake*," and the south wind to "come." He knows exactly what each member can bear—the requisite pruning for each branch—the *look* which will soften a Peter's heart—the *reproof* that will convince the unbelieving Thomas—the *sympathy* which will bind up the bleeding hearts of the bereaved sisters of Bethany, &c. &c. And all is administered by the Spirit. "All these worketh that one and the self-same Spirit, dividing to every man severally as he will" (1 Cor. xii. 11).

Where he works, too, he works *effectually*; the spices will flow out, the odour of a sweet smell.

" Blow upon my garden." The words are the words of Jesus, for the garden is *his* alone. " *My* garden " — I have purchased it with mine own blood ; it is mine : therefore I will send forth from my Father " the Spirit of life," that he may *breathe* upon it. " The Spirit of God moved (Heb., ' breathed ') upon the face of the waters " (Gen. i. 2). " Blow upon my garden, that the spices thereof may flow out."

On Chapter iv. 12-15.

" We are a garden wall'd around,
Chosen and made peculiar ground ;
A little spot inclosed by grace,
Out of the world's wide wilderness.

" Like trees of myrrh and spice we stand,
Planted by God the Father's hand ;
And all his springs in Zion flow,
To make the young plantation grow.

" Awake, O heavenly Wind ! and come,
Blow on this garden of perfume ;
Spirit Divine ! descend and breathe
A gracious gale on plants beneath."—Watts.

The Bride.

" *Let my beloved come into his garden, and eat his pleasant fruits.*"

There are seasons, when the soul is under the special culture of the Spirit, that call forth such language as this from the children of God. They are so sensible that the garden is Christ's—not theirs

—and that the fruits are the fruits of his own Spirit
in them, and nothing of their own, that they can in
all humility invite the Lord of heaven and earth,
the King of kings, the Lord of lords, yea, they can
invite him as the *beloved* of their souls, to come in
and sup with them, and make his abode with them,
" and eat his pleasant fruits."

They do not deny that the fruits of grace in their
souls are " pleasant ;" they do not question their
worthiness to receive such a guest ; but, in the
intense longings of their souls after closer communion with him, they gladly invite him to come
in : " Let my beloved *come into* his garden." It is a
false, untrue humility, to deny the great things
which God hath wrought in us. Thus we read
that St Paul " *declared particularly* what things God
had wrought *by his* ministry" (Acts xxi. 19) ; and
in writing to Philemon (ver. 6), he says, " that the
communication of thy faith may become effectual
by *the acknowledging* of every good thing which is
in you in Christ Jesus." (See also Ps. lxvi. 16 ;
1 Cor. xv. 10.)

It only becomes us most carefully to see that
we call the garden " *his*," and the fruits " *his*," dis-
claiming anything like merit or aught that is good
in ourselves — " in me dwelleth no good thing."
" Let my beloved come into his garden, and eat his
pleasant fruits." They are his; let him have all
the glory; let him accept and use them, and be
glorified and *satisfied* in them. (See John xv. 8.)

" The fruits of righteousness are *by* Jesus Christ " (Phil. i. 11). The good things are wrought by " *God* " (Acts xxi. 19), and every good thing which is in us is so " *in Christ Jesus* " (Philemon 6). No works of ours could be pleasant to the Lord, for the best are tainted with sin, and he can " eat " nothing that is unclean.

" But the greatest delight that Christ hath in the world, is in the garden of his Church ; therefore, that he might take *full* delight therein, he makes it fruitful, stored with precious fruits, growing from plants set by his own hand, relished of his own Spirit, and so fitted to his taste."—ROWBOTHAM.

And to prove how acceptable the prayer of his Bride was, he answers it by immediately acceding to her request.

CHAPTER V.

CHRIST'S ANSWER.

Ver. 1. " *I am come into my garden, my sister, my spouse; I have gathered my myrrh with my spice; I have eaten my honeycomb with my honey; I have drunk my wine with my milk.*"

Already "I am come!" A God at hand, with his ears always attent unto the prayers of his people.

There is something very striking in the oneness of sentiment and even language pervading this book, sweetly telling that "*we have* the mind of Christ" (1 Cor. ii. 16). Thus the Bride had called him her "Beloved" (chap. iv. 16); now he calls her "my sister, my spouse." She called it "his garden," and he owns it as such—"I am come into *my* garden." She invited him to "eat his pleasant fruits," and he says, "I *have* eaten," &c. *He* also, most emphatically, calls them all his own : "I have gathered *my* myrrh with *my* spice; I have eaten *my* honeycomb with *my* honey; I have drunk *my* wine

with *my* milk." We have nothing of our own ; all
we have and are is the Lord's (1 Cor. vi. 19, 20).
" What hast thou that thou didst not receive ?"
(1 Cor. iv. 7.)

We see, too, how ready Jesus is to accept *what
each has to offer.* From one plant he gathers
" myrrh "—fitly representing, by its bitterness, the
tears of godly sorrow shed by the repenting sinner,
when convinced of sin by the piercing blasts of the
" *north* wind."

From another he gathers " honey," and the
honeycomb — intimating, from its sweetness, the
manifestation of the mild and gentle graces of the
Spirit, called into exercise by the blowing of the
" *south* " wind.

From another he gathers " spice ;" from the
young Christian, " milk ;" and from the aged and
matured believer, " wine ;" for milk belongs to the
babe in Christ, but strong meat to them that are of
full age (Heb. v. 13, 14). All are alike accepted
of Jesus, the bitter and the sweet, the young and
the old ; and, yet more, all are sources of delight
and enjoyment to him. He actually *feeds* upon the
graces of the Spirit in the hearts of his people, for
he says, " I have *eaten!* I have *drunk!* " How
feebly we realise this wonderful truth !

But our Beloved not only feasts thereon himself, but even calls us to feast with him, and to be
sharers of his joy.

" *Eat, O friends ; drink, yea, drink abundantly, O
   beloved.*"

"Eat ye that which is good, and let your soul
delight itself in fatness "—" Except ye eat the flesh
of the Son of man, and drink his blood, ye have no
life in you. For my flesh is meat indeed, and my
blood is drink indeed" (Isa. lv. 1, 2 ; John vi.
53–57). " Eat, O friends." Christ would have
believers partake of the soul-refreshing blessings
of his purchase. " Whosoever will, let him take
the water of life freely." " They drank of that
spiritual Rock that followed them, and that Rock
was Christ " (Rev. xxii. 17 ; 1 Cor. x. 4). " Drink
abundantly," or, as it is in the margin, " be *drunken*
with loves ; " " be *filled* with the Spirit, and not
with wine," says the apostle (Eph. v. 18). There
is no danger of excess in this spiritual feast; we
cannot spiritually eat too much of the flesh, nor
drink too much of the blood, of the Lord Jesus.
" Eat, yea, *drink abundantly.*"

This involves the inexhaustible nature of the
provision made for us. All may eat, and all may
drink, and yet there shall be " enough and to
spare."

There is also comfort in the expression "*friends.*"
" I have not called you servants, but *friends* " (John
xv. 15). It bespeaks an intimacy between Christ
and his people, of no ordinary kind. They " *sup* "
together (Rev. iii. 20). As in the peace-offering of
old, God, the offerer, and the priests, were all fed

by it, so in Jesus, *our peace-offering* (Eph. ii. 14), the Father, the Son, and his friends all partake. This is communion—"Truly our fellowship is with the Father, and with his Son, Jesus Christ" (1 John i. 3).

> "Thrice happy he, who here partakes
> That sacred stream, that heavenly food."—DODDRIDGE.

Chapter v. 1 seems more properly to belong to the 4th chapter, as it follows in immediate connection with the verse preceding it, and forms a beautiful conclusion to the words of Christ to his Bride ; for that chapter is throughout the expression of the complacent love of Jesus towards her : it emphatically describes the *summer season* of the soul's experience, and in this verse she is called to share in his joy.

But here this happy, blessed season closes. We know no *uninterrupted* communion yet. By reason of the frailty of our nature, we cannot always stand upright; and one chief part of our discipline consists in "*the trial* of our *faith*." It must be *sifted*, to prove its reality ; and it frequently happens that the great enemy of souls makes his most successful attempts upon us immediately after seasons of peculiar enjoyment. It was thus with the Bride on this occasion.

Ver. 2. "*I sleep, but my heart waketh.*"

Very, very humbling is it to meet with repeated instances of declension in every believer's walk ;

yet so it is. The Bride is here just like the disciples, who, the very night in which they had partaken of the Lord's Supper, and when they so especially ought to have been *watching, were asleep* (Matt. xxvi. 40, 43).

" I sleep, but my heart waketh." *Asleep*—in a state of stupor, inactivity, and insecurity. No girding on of the Christian armour—no fighting the good fight of faith—no " watching unto prayer "—neither hot nor cold, but in a state of lukewarmness like that of the Laodicean Church (Rev. iii.) Still it is " sleep," not death ; for the believer in Jesus cannot die. Though dead to all *sense* of life, he still lives, for Christ lives in him.

" I sleep, *but* my heart waketh." That " *but*' is a precious indication of life ; it implies *restless* sleep—" But my heart waketh." There is also the distinct recognition, in these words, of the Christian conflict between the flesh and the spirit ; the one warring against the other. The flesh asleep, the spirit wakeful—" *I* sleep, but *my heart* waketh." (Compare Rom. vii. and Gal. v.)

" The spirit truly is willing, but the flesh is weak."

" As natural sleep proceedeth from weariness of the body, so spiritual sleep ariseth from too much expense of the strength of the soul upon matters of the world."—Rowbotham.

" *It is the voice of my beloved that knocketh, saying,*

Open to me, my sister, my love, my dove, my un-defiled."

This restlessness was not the result of any *effort* of the Church; believers cannot rouse *themselves* when they fall asleep, any more than sinners can give life to their dead souls. It was the knock of Christ that woke the sleeping Bride. " It is the voice of my beloved that knocketh." *He* neither slumbers nor sleeps. He is watching his sleeping children when drowsiness comes over their souls, *as truly* as he watches over their dust when it is laid in their graves until the morning of the resurrection. Like Hagar in the wilderness, we have still one who looks after us (Gen. xvi. 7–14). " Behold, I stand at the door and knock," was his tender language to the sleeping Church of Laodicea. " Awake, thou that sleepest " (Eph. v. 14)—" What meanest thou, O sleeper ? *arise*, call upon thy God " (Jonah i. 6). When the disciples were sleeping in the garden, Jesus did not sleep ; nay, it was *for them* he sweat those great drops of blood. And *twice* he goeth to them, and yet a *third* time, and finds them sleeping, and then he *knocks*, and says, " Rise, let us be going " (Matt. xxvi. 36, &c.)

" It is the voice of my beloved "—the voice that shall one day *be heard* by all that are in their graves (John v. 28, 29) ; and oh ! what will it not *then* be to us to be able to call him *"my beloved !"* The Bride heard and recognised his voice, and all the tender words he spake to her : " It is the voice of my beloved that knocketh, *saying*, Open to me, my sister, my love, my dove, my undefiled."

And is it *thus* that Jesus speaks to a soul in such a state as this? Is he not angry and displeased with her? Will he not sharply rebuke and reprove her? Can he address her still as his sister, his undefiled? Then surely nothing can so plainly prove to the believer, that, let his own feelings be what they may, *the love of Jesus towards him never for one moment changes*, even in seasons of deepest backsliding. *Still* he owns his people in their *covenant relationship*. Oh! the precious comfort of *such* expressions *at such a moment!*—"My sister, my love, my dove, my undefiled."

"Open to me"—"to *me*." Shut not the door against *me*—"I am *Jesus*, whom thou persecutest." Remember against *whom* thou art kicking—"Me," thy brother, thy friend, thy beloved! "Is this thy kindness to thy friend?"

> "*For my head is filled with dew, and my locks with the drops of the night.*"

What an argument!—"Open to me, *for* my head is filled with dew." Will not such a recollection move thee? Canst thou recall my sufferings for thee *unmoved?* Think of that night, that dreadful night, when my sweat was as it were great drops of blood, through the intensity of my sufferings for thee! No storm on the darkest night could picture the agony that found vent in that bitter cry, wrung

from sinking humanity, " My God, my God, why
hast thou forsaken me ? " The outward darkness
that overspread the earth for three hours gave but
the faintest representation of the dark season of inward desertion which accompanied it ; " I cry in the
night season, but thou hearest not " (Ps. xxii. 1, 2).
" My head is filled with dew, and my locks with the
drops of the night "—those pelting " drops" of the
Father's fury and wrath, which burst upon his head
when he stood *accursed* as the sinner's substitute.
Can we withstand such love ? Can we resist that
voice ? Can we suffer Jesus to be *standing without,*
and not rise and open to him ?

> " Lo ! Gethsemane *in night !*
>   Vengeance there with iron rod,
> Stood, and with collected might,
>   Bruised the harmless Lamb of God :
> See, my soul, the Saviour see,
> Suffering in Gethsemane !
>
> " *View* thy Maker's deep distress,
>   *Hear* the sighs and groans of God," &c.—HART.

It is *His* voice that speaks, and speaks *to thee ;* he
who " endured the cross, despising the shame," whose
head was crowned with thorns—*He* says, " Open to
me."

Ver. 3. " *I have put off my coat ; how shall I put it
on ? I have washed my feet ; how shall I defile
them ?* "

Alas ! that Jesus should ever get such a return for
such love ! Instead of opening at once to her Beloved,

the Bride only gives way to indolent excuses. She is not yet half aroused from her lethargy—" I have put off my coat; how shall I put it on? I have washed my feet; how shall I defile them?" The Christian armour is laid aside, and now she shrinks from the conflict; her feet are washed (referring to the custom in Eastern countries of washing the feet before lying down to rest, as, from wearing no shoes, they became soiled at every step), how shall she again expose herself to the defilements of the way? How often a child of God, who has fallen into declension, hears warnings and invitations unheeded! " I cannot pray now; God will not hear me. I have no desires after Him; I shrink from the conflict as men 'averse from war' (Mic. ii. 8); I cannot put on those garments which I have laid aside," &c.

It is the language of *despair*, as well as of indolence—" *How can I?*" (Deut. vii. 17–19.) But it is sometimes well when the child of God is brought to this; for truly we are not sufficient of ourselves to think anything *as of ourselves*. And when we *feel* our utter inability, God often manifests *his power*.

Ver. 4. " *My beloved put in his hand by the hole of the door, and my bowels were moved for him.*"

When we will not hear *the voice* which speaks, it sometimes pleases God to lay *his hand* upon us. " Thy hand presseth me sore" (Ps. xxxviii. 2)—even that right hand which is glorious in power (Ex. xv.

6). For he does not easily give us up (see Hos. xi. 7, 8) ; and though the door be shut, and we refuse to rise and open it, there is still a way of entrance left to *Him* who knows "the *secrets of the heart*" (Ps. xliv. 21). "My beloved put in his hand by the hole of the door." In many unexpected ways he finds access to the believer's heart. It was so with Peter, who heeded it not though Jesus *told* him that ere the cock crew he would deny him thrice ; but so soon as "the Lord *turned and looked* upon him," at once his bowels were moved, "and he went out and wept bitterly" (Luke xxii. 61, 62). Jesus had, as it were, knocked in vain, but now "he put in his hand by the hole of the door," *and thus let himself in !*

> Ver. 5. "*I rose up to open to my beloved ; and my hands dropped with myrrh, and my fingers with sweet-smelling myrrh, upon the handles of the lock.*"

Such are the blessed effects of the dealings of the Lord Jesus with the soul—"I *rose up.*" For that ye sorrowed after a godly sort, what carefulness it wrought in you ; yea, what clearing of yourselves ; yea, what zeal ; yea, what vehement desire, &c. (2 Cor. vii. 11.) And, oh ! what bitter, bitter tears the child of God will shed over the hindrances which have locked out Jesus from his heart !—tears of penitence and deep contrition for his sins, mingled with tears of gratitude to him whose hand unlocked that closed door. "My hands dropped with myrrh, and my fingers with sweet-smelling myrrh." Even the bitterness is sweet. The child of God knows more of true happiness in seeking Jesus with many tears, than in idly keeping at a distance from him. Mary is a striking instance of this. Her "many sins," instead of keeping her away from him, brought her nigh *to bathe his feet with her tears.* And those tears were *sweet* to Jesus (see Luke vii. 44–47).

The sins, "the handles of the lock," that close the door against the Beloved of our souls, will be bitterly repented of. But that repentance is a grace of the Spirit that comes up with acceptance to Jesus from his garden, with the odour of a sweet smell. "Sweet-smelling myrrh."

Ver. 6. "*I opened to my beloved ; but my beloved had withdrawn himself, and was gone.*"

Such experience is peculiar to true believers. For whilst the Lord withdraws the sense of his pre-sence from the indolent and slothful *child,* he never deals so with a soul that is but *seeking after him* at the first stage of the divine life. Such an one would be thereby driven to despair, while the former is but stirred up to more diligent search. He knows the exact measure of faith in his people, and the degree of trial which that faith requires ; therefore he will not suffer any one to be tempted (or *tried*) above what they are *able to bear.* The Bride had reluctantly opened to her Beloved, but not till he had been com-pelled to lay his hand upon her, because she heeded not his voice. She must, therefore, learn that it is

an evil and a bitter thing to requite him thus (Jer.
ii. 19) ; and he will not at once grant her the former
experience she had enjoyed in the realising sense of
his presence : " My beloved had withdrawn himself,
and was gone."

Still, the *sense* of his absence proved that she had
already known the sweetness of his presence ; she
was no stranger to him. She was now deprived of
what she had before enjoyed, and being thoroughly
awake, she *feels* what she had lost while she slept.

It is deeply painful to realise, through *returning
consciousness* after sleep in spiritual things, what a
loss we have sustained. Our sensible enjoyment of
the presence of Jesus is "*gone*,"—" my beloved had
withdrawn himself, and was gone ;" that is, the sensible manifestation of himself, for if he had really
left her, she certainly would have had no desire after
him. But to quicken us, and arouse us from our
lethargy and indifference, he lets us feel what it is
to be without a felt sense of his presence. And every
child of God who knows what this experience is. can
testify, that a sense of the absence of one so dear is
more than they can bear, especially if it be from
their own repeated provocations (Jer. ii. 17). They
know no rest until they find him.

" *My soul failed when he spake.*"

" My soul *failed*." This is a very strong word,
being the same that is elsewhere rendered "their
heart *went forth*" (Gen. xlii. 28, margin), intimat-

ing the most intense dismay and anguish. And
thus it fitly expresses that deep, poignant sorrow
experienced by the soul until the cloud is passed
which hides the light of God's countenance : " My
soul failed when he spake." She hears his voice (or,
as the Hebrew may be rendered, calls his neglected
words to remembrance), but she cannot realise his
presence with her. Nothing else can satisfy her,
and yet she has not *that.* " O that I were as in
months past," is her language, " as in the days when
God preserved me, when his candle shined upon my
head ! " (Job xxix. 2, 3.) " Hear me speedily, O Lord,
my spirit faileth ; hide not thy face from me "—" I
had fainted unless I had believed to see the goodness
of the Lord," &c. (Ps. cxliii. 7 ; xxvii. 13.)

It argues strong faith in the Bride, that she should
still be seeking after Christ, though in such utter
want of enjoyment ; and he deals with her accord-
ingly. " The strong he'll strongly try."

> " *I sought him, but I could not find him ; I called
> him, but he gave me no answer.*"

So also Job says, " O that I knew where I might
find him ! Behold, I go forward, but he is not there ;
and backward, but I cannot perceive him," &c. (Job
xxiii. 3–9 ; see also Job xxxiv. 29). But the true
believer still *goes on seeking,* though the heavens seem
as brass, and though his bitter cry is, " Thou hast
covered thyself with a cloud, that our prayer should
not pass through ;" "also when I cry and shout, he

shutteth out my prayer" (Lament. iii. 8, 44)—"I called him, but he gave me no answer"—"I cry unto thee, and thou dost not hear me" (Job xxx. 20).

It was thus also with the poor woman of Canaan, who came to Jesus earnestly entreating him to heal her daughter—"*but he answered her not a word!*" (see Matt. xv. 22, 23.) "I called him, but he gave me no answer."

And wherefore did he deal so with her? "For the trial of her faith," doubtless; for it is thus the Lord suits his dealing to the peculiar requirements of his people. Their trials are divinely adapted trials, and there is grace divinely adapted to their need *in* their trials. It was the *strong faith* in the Bride and in the Canaanitish woman, which *justified* (so to speak) this severe trial of it. They *were* "able to bear" it. And the contrast in the case of the poor woman who "came behind him trembling," fully confirms this. The strong faith is exercised with long delay, while the weak, trembling faith receives a word of *immediate* comfort. (See Luke viii. 44, 47, 48). Let us therefore learn to "trust him where we cannot trace."

But we should learn also, as has been beautifully remarked, "that, while there is forgiveness with the Lord, it should be esteemed by us no light thing to be drawing on that forgiveness. For, while it is true that 'forgive us our trespasses' may be said by the children of God in spirit *continually*, knowing as

they must in how many things they all offend, it is
still a serious thing to be drawing on the pardoning
grace of God. The Book of Judges illustrates this,
shewing a *growing reserve* on the part of God towards
His people. As they repeat their demands on his
grace, He holds himself more and more distant from
them."

The experience of the Bride is precisely similar.
Compare chap. iii. 1, 4, where the search was comparatively easy (as she was so much more ready to
commence it), with chap. v. 2–8, where her re-
luctance to rise and open to her Beloved caused
such delay in her finding him. "I sought him,
but I could not find him; I called him, but he
gave me no answer."

Believer, if at any time while thou art engaged
in earnestly calling upon God, he answers thee "not
a word," mark what that delay says to thee —
"*Great is thy faith!*"

> Ver. 7. "*The watchmen that went about the city
> found me, they smote me, they wounded me; the
> keepers of the walls took away my vail from me.*"

It appears that during the Bride's search for her
Beloved she met with reproach and severe treat-
ment from the ministers of the Lord. For they are
the watchmen; "they watch for your souls as they
that must give account" (Heb. xiii. 17). The word
of the Lord in their mouths seems to have been like
a sharp "two-edged sword, piercing even to the divid-

ing asunder of soul and spirit," &c., and "like *a hammer* that breaketh the rock in pieces" (Heb. iv. 12 ; Jer. xxiii. 29). "They smote me, they wounded me." The word came home with such convincing power, that it wounded her to the quick. It was sharp reproof, for the watchmen prophesied not "smooth things," but stripped her of all the filthy rags of her own righteousness, and disclosed her sad condition. It was very painful, and very humbling, but it worked for "good" in the end. " Let the righteous smite me, it shall be a kindness; and let him reprove me, it shall be an excellent oil which shall not break my head" (Ps. cxli. 5).

Ver. 8. " *I charge you, O daughters of Jerusalem, if ye find my beloved, that ye tell him, that I am sick of love*" (Greek, " *wounded with love*").

The Bride gets more and more earnest. She can no longer keep her anxiety to herself; she must speak of it to every one she meets ; she must ask their prayers (for it is evidently prayer that is meant by the expression " *tell him* "). Speak to my Beloved for me : tell him my sad case. " I beseech you, brethren, for the Lord Jesus Christ's sake, and for the love of the Spirit, that *ye* strive together with me, *in your prayers* to God *for me* " (Rom xv. 30). " For I know that this shall turn to my salvation *through your prayer*," &c.—" Pray one for another" (Phil i. 19 ; James v. 16).

The Bride could not speak confidently as to the

successful use of means in this case ; it is only, " *if*
ye find him."   Still she would leave no means un-
tried ; and her earnestness betrayed such sincerity
of love, and such utter dissatisfaction with everything short of Christ, that *even her soul sickness*
testified to the daughters of Jerusalem what a
powerful reality there is in true vital godliness.
They at once inquire—

> Ver. 9. " *What is thy beloved more than another*
> *beloved, O thou fairest among women ?   What is*
> *thy beloved more than another beloved, that thou*
> *dost so charge us ?*"

Their question plainly proved their ignorance of
Jesus, for they saw " no beauty in him that they
should desire him."   The veil was still upon their
hearts ; the god of this world still blinded their
eyes.   But it was well that they were brought to
inquire after him.   " What is thy beloved more
than another beloved, that thou dost so charge us ?"
What is the peculiar superiority in the object of
your affections above ours ?   Alas ! how many idols,
how many *other beloveds* are there, that take God's
place in the soul !—love of the world and the things
that are therein—love of *the creature* more than the
Creator, &c. &c.   " Strange gods "—*other beloveds!*
But when Christ is truly known, he is " among the
sons " as the apple-tree among the wild trees of the
wood (chap. ii. 3).   The Bride had expressly appro-
priated him to herself — " if ye find *my* beloved ;"

and they at once acknowledge him to have been hers in a sense in which they knew him not. " What is *thy* beloved more than another beloved ?" They seem to have been especially struck with two things : first, the Bride's own beauty, and, secondly, her deep earnestness. Her renown had gone forth for her beauty (Ezek. xvi. 14). The holiness which is (or should be) stamped upon every member of the Church of Christ, was visible in her. For they called her the " fairest among women." How strange that they should so clearly discover the beauty of Jesus *in her*, and yet not know *him* (from whom all her beauty came) as " fairer than the children of men"! (Ps. xlv. 2.)

But, secondly, the charge the Bride had given them, *and her manner of giving it*, had impressed these professors. " What is thy beloved more than another beloved, that thou dost *so* charge us ?"—so earnestly—so vehemently ! Surely there must be something here that we don't understand—something *more* than *we* know !

Oh ! what encouragement this affords to poor, tried, disconsolate believers, who are walking in darkness, and have no light ! Jesus can make their diligent search for him, in such seasons, as great a means of leading others to inquire after him, as their happiest moments of privileged communion. Sometimes, it may be, when we are least aware of it, we may be most used by the Lord to accomplish his great work. Our very dissatisfaction with

everything short of Christ, may be the very means
chosen to make others see a worth and inestimable
value in him, of which those who are content with
lesser beloveds know nothing.   Truly,

> " God moves in a mysterious way,
>   His wonders to perform ! "

The double repetition of the inquiry made by
the daughters of Jerusalem was indicative of a real
desire on their parts to know something more of
Jesus ; and it becomes the Christian to "be *ready
always* to *give an answer* to every man that asketh
a reason of the hope that is in him."   This the Bride
was.   For she immediately bursts forth into a holy
strain of glorying in the Lord—boasting of his
exceeding excellency. and the superiority of *his*
person far above *all others*.

Ver. 10. " *My beloved is white and ruddy.*"

There is a beauty in him such as can be found
in none besides.   He is " white and ruddy ;" or, as
Fry renders it, " fair and blooming."   He is always
so : there is, as it were, the blooming immortality
of an eternal spring in Jesus—" the same, yesterday,
to-day, and for ever."

It is recorded of David, as a youth, that he
was " ruddy and of a fair countenance " (1 Sam.
xvii. 42) ; and how much more so the true David
—the true Beloved ! (The word David means *beloved*.)   " My beloved is white and ruddy "—white,
as " the lily of the valley "—ruddy, as " the rose of

Sharon." "*White*," for he is the Lamb "without blemish and without spot"—"holy, harmless, undefiled, and separate from sinners" (1 Pet. i. 18, 19; Exod. xii. 5; Heb. vii. 26). In him was no darkness at all. When Daniel saw him, it was as "the Ancient of days, whose garment was *white as snow*, and the hair of his head *like the pure wool*." When John saw him, "his head and his hairs were *white* like wool, *as white as snow*." And when the disciples saw him in the mount of transfiguration, "his face did shine as the sun, and his raiment was *white as the light!*" (Dan. vii. 9; Rev. i. 14; Matt. xvii. 2.) None was ever pure and white like Jesus!

He is ruddy also; for he is "the Lamb *slain* from the foundation of the world"—the paschal lamb, whose blood, "the blood of the everlasting covenant," is sprinkled on the door-posts of every believer's heart. Even "in the midst of the throne" he is still seen, "a lamb *as it had been slain*" (Rev. v. 6). And in a yet coming day, he shall appear "clothed with a vesture dipped in blood"—"*red* in thine apparel, and thy garments like him that treadeth in the wine-fat!" (Rev. xix. 13; Isa. lxiii. 1-3.) None was ever clad in a blood-dyed garment like Jesus!

"*The chiefest among ten thousand*" (margin, "*a standard-bearer*").

"Who in the heaven can be compared unto the Lord? Who among the sons of the mighty can be

likened unto the Lord?" (Ps. lxxxix. 6.) "Thou
art fairer than the children of men : thou lovest
righteousness, and hatest wickedness ; therefore
God, thy God, hath anointed thee with the oil of
gladness *above thy fellows* (Ps. xlv. 2, 7). None was
ever so lovely, so exalted as Jesus ! God has given
him as " a Leader and Commander to the people "
—their " Ensign " and their " Forerunner " (Isa. lv.
4 ; xi. 10 ; Heb. vi. 20)—" *The Captain of their salvation* " (Heb. ii. 10).

And the language of our hearts should ever be
what the men of war said of old to David, " *Thou
art worth ten thousand of us* " (2 Sam. xviii. 3).
" The chiefest among ten thousand ! " The " Alpha
and Omega " (Rev. i. 8)—" The *First-born* of every
creature " (Col. i. 15–18)—The " Pearl of *great*
price " (Matt. xiii. 46) — " A *great* High Priest "
(Heb. iv. 14)—" That *great* Shepherd of the sheep "
(Heb. xiii. 20)—" The *great* God," &c. (Titus ii. 13)
—" A *great* Rock in a weary land " (Isa. xxxii. 2)—
the "greater than Solomon " (Matt. xii. 42)—" The
Prince of the kings of the earth" (Rev. i. 5)—" The
chief Shepherd" (1 Pet. v. 4)—" A *chief* corner-
stone " (1 Pet. ii. 6)—" The *First-born* among *many*
brethren " (Rom. viii. 29). Surely " God hath
highly exalted him, and given him a name which is
above every name, that at the name of Jesus every
knee should bow," &c. (Phil. ii. 9–11).

As Newton has beautifully expressed it :—

" As by the light of opening day
The stars are all conceal'd,
So *creature*-pleasures fade away
When *Jesus* is reveal'd."

" My beloved is white and ruddy ; the chiefest
among ten thousand."

" Yes ! my Beloved to my sight
Shews a sweet mixture—red and white ;
All human beauties, all divine,
In my Beloved meet and shine.
White is his soul, from blemish free,
Red with the blood he shed for me.
The fairest of ten thousand fairs,
The sun among ten thousand stars."—WATTS.

But the Bride is not content with this general
commendation of the excellencies of Jesus. He did
not so easily weary of *her* beauty (see chap. iv.) ;
neither will she of *his*. She delights *in himself*, *in
his person*, in all that *he is*. She cannot say enough
to express what she finds in him. And truly it is
deeply humbling that we can enter so little into her
experience. The work and offices of their Lord are
the most that many Christians ever know of him.
His death, resurrection, and intercession are enough
for them ; a believing apprehension of these divine
mysteries secures their eternal safety, and they but
seldom go on to the contemplation of all that Jesus
is in his personal glory—his humanity—" *His own
self* " (1 Pet. ii. 24).

Consequently this precious book, which dwells so
largely on this blessed theme, is but little prized and
relished. The Lord lead us into a deeper conviction
of his own exceeding excellencies, that we may

realise what a portion we have in him *now*, and that we may ardently look for his return, when " we shall see him *as he is!* "

> " The more *Thy* glories strike mine eyes,
>   The lower *I* shall lie ;
> Thus while I sink, my joy shall rise
>   Unmeasurably high."—WATTS.

Ver. 11. " *His head is as the most fine gold.*"

The most precious things the world contains are those chosen to set forth the worth of Jesus. " The most fine gold " (Heb. " gold of gold "). And this is spoken of the *head* of Jesus, that sacred head once crowned with thorns, once laid in a manger,—" for the Son of man had not where to lay his head." But God hath " made him to be head over all things." " He is the head of the body, . . . that in all things he might have the pre-eminence " (Eph. i. 22 ; Col. i. 18 ; Ps. cx. 7).

We are reminded, too, *of the Godhead* of Christ —" The head of Christ is God " (1 Cor. xi. 3) ; and of his sovereignty, even as Nebuchadnezzar was represented as king of kings, by " a head of gold " (Dan. ii. 32, 38).

The double expression, " gold, gold," may have reference to the two words which are used in the original to signify gold—one, implying its shining brightness and brilliancy ; the other, its firmness and solidity. And thus the very height of excellency would be intended in the figure.

" His head the finest gold excels,
There wisdom in perfection dwells;
And glory like a crown adorns
Those temples once beset with thorns."—WATTS.

" And on his head were many crowns." Truly
Jesus shall ever be found *a golden possession* to all
who can claim him as their Beloved !

" *His locks are bushy, and black as a raven.*"

The word rendered " black " is elsewhere translated " youth " (see Eccles. xi. 10); so that the idea
chiefly suggested in these words is the vigour of
youth. " His locks are bushy, and black as a
raven." There are no " gray hairs " to be found upon
our Jesus (see Hos. vii. 9). While others are waxing
old like a garment, he is ever " the *same*," and his
years to all generations (Ps. cii. 27).

The mention of a " *raven*" in such immediate
contrast to the *dove* (ver. 12), is as remarkable as the
preceding verse—" My beloved is *white* and *ruddy*."
Such wonders, and (to our finite understandings)
opposite attributes, are to be found combined in our
God. With the simplicity of the dove is to be seen
the impenetrable darkness of the raven : " black as
a raven." " His judgments are very deep." " Clouds
and darkness are round about him." " His path is
in the sea, and his footsteps are not known." He is
" *past finding out.*" " He will render judgment to
his enemies," for " he is strong in power "—" *wisdom*
and *might* are his " (Rom. xi. 33 ; Ps. xcvii. 2 ; Isa.
xl. 26 ; Dan. ii. 20).

There is none so omnipotent as Jesus !

Ver. 12. " *His eyes are as the eyes of doves by the rivers of waters, washed with milk, and fitly set*" (margin, " *sitting in fulness* ").

" The eyes of the Lord are in every place, behold-ing the evil and the good "—" All things are naked and opened unto the eyes of him with whom we have to do " (Prov. xv. 3 ; Heb. iv. 13). And there is nothing terrible in this to the believer, for " his eyes are as the eyes of *doves*," full of tenderness, gentleness, and affection. If his eyes run to and fro throughout the whole earth, it is that he may shew himself strong *in behalf* of them whose heart is per-fect toward him (2 Chron. xvi. 9). It is an un-speakable comfort to the children of God to know that " the eyes of the Lord are over the righteous," and that he is always sitting by as the refiner, *to watch* the gold in the furnace.

What looks of delight and complacency beam from the eyes of Jesus towards his people ! from those eyes, which once *wept* tears of grief over Jeru-salem—which were " lifted up " to meet the down-ward glance of his Father's eye, in prayer for his people (John xvii. 1)—and which " looked upon Peter " with such inimitable tenderness ! (Luke xxii. 61 ; see also Ps. xxxii. 8 ; Ex. iii. 7, 8 ; Mark iii. 34 ; Luke xix. 5.)

Their being " set in fulness " is strikingly set forth in Rev. v. 6—" a lamb . . . . . having seven horns and *seven eyes* "—seven denoting fulness, completeness, and perfection (see also Zech. iii. 9, and iv. 10).

There is none so *omniscient* as Jesus!

(Compare " doves by the rivers of waters," with Mat. iii. 16.)

Ver. 13. " *His cheeks are as a bed of spices, as sweet flowers*" (margin, " *Towers of perfumes*").

Literally, his *face*, or *countenance*. All fragrance, sweetness, and beauty, are at once combined " in the face of Jesus Christ"—that face which was once shamefully entreated, and spitted on, as it is written, " I hid not my face from shame and spitting; I gave my cheeks to them that plucked off the hair" (Isa. l. 6). But the believer finds it his highest delight to walk in the light of that countenance (Ps. iv. 6; lxxxix. 15). It is like walking beside " a bed of spices; " not, as it were, one flower here or there, but " *a bed* of spices"—*a mass* of " sweet flowers," filling the air with fragrance.

" *His lips like lilies, dropping sweet-smelling myrrh.*"

" Grace is poured into thy lips" (Ps. xlv. 2). His lips were ever ready to drop sweetness, for "never man spake like this man!" " He will *speak peace* unto his people, and to his saints" (John vii. 46; Ps. lxxxv. 8). " The words that I speak unto you, they are spirit, and they are life"—for " the Lord God hath given me the tongue of the learned, that I

I

should know how to speak *a word in season* to him that is weary" (John vi. 63 ; Isa. l. 4). Who can tell the efficacy of those " gracious words that proceed out of his mouth" ? " *Speak the word only*, and my servant shall be healed."

Very sweet were the words of comfort the Lord Jesus was wont to drop, from time to time, as he went about doing good ;—to a bereaved widow, " Weep not" (Luke vii. 13) ; to the poor woman who came behind him trembling to touch only the border of his garment, " Daughter, be of good comfort ; go in peace" (Luke viii. 48) ; to the ruler of the synagogue, when the heart-rending intelligence of his child's death reached him, " Be not afraid, only believe" (Mark v. 36) ; to the disciples, when they " cried out for fear," and were troubled, because they saw (as they thought) a spirit walking on the sea, " Be of good cheer ; *it is I*, be not afraid" (Matt. xiv. 24–27).

And yet those lips were accused of speaking " blasphemy !"

Ver. 14. " *His hands are as gold rings set with the beryl.*"

" The beryl is a green stone, which never receives reflection from any other colour or shade, but remains unaffected by contact with other things." — Mrs Stevens.

The beryl set in golden rings seems, therefore, to represent the *perfection* of the works of his hands.

Nothing can be added to them, nothing taken from them.

"His work is perfect"—"The works of his hands are verity and judgment: they stand fast for ever and ever, and are done in truth and uprightness" (Deut. xxxii. 4; Ps. cxi. 7, 8). "O Lord, how manifold are thy works! in wisdom hast thou made them all" (Ps. civ. 24). "Excellent in working" (Isa. xxviii. 29).

> "His hands are fairer to behold
> Than diamonds set in rings of gold;
> Those heavenly hands that on the tree
> Were nail'd, and torn, and bled for me."—WATTS.

When Peter was ready to sink, "immediately Jesus stretched forth his hand, and caught him" (Matt. xiv. 31); when a man "full of leprosy" came and besought him to heal him, Jesus, without heeding the loathsomeness of the disease, "put forth his hand, and *touched* him" (Luke v. 13); and when a blind man was brought to him, he took him by the hand and led him out of the town, *and once and again* he laid his hands upon him, until he was restored, and saw every man clearly (Mark viii. 22–25); whilst to the unbelieving Thomas he said, "Reach hither thy finger, *and behold my hands!*" &c., the hands once pierced with nails! (John xx. 20–27.)

Oh! how precious the security of the Church of Christ, graven on the palms of his hands (Isa. xlix. 16), even those hands whence none shall pluck the least lamb in his fold! (John x. 29); "in whose hand are all the corners of the earth," and who

" hath measured the waters in the hollow of his hand !" (Isa. xl. 12.)   Oh ! how sweet to have that upholding hand under our head, and his right hand embracing us !   How sweet to be enclosed within those golden rings !

" *His belly is as bright ivory overlaid with sapphires.*"

" His bowels (as the word is everywhere else rendered) are as bright ivory overlaid with sapphires ;" the bowels of his compassion.   " My *bowels* are troubled for him : I will surely have mercy upon him, saith the Lord"—" Mine *heart* is turned within me ; my repentings are kindled together" (Jer. xxxi. 20 ; Hos. xi. 8; see also Isa. lxiii. 15).   The expression bespeaks the depth of the riches of his tenderness and love.   It commends *the heart* of Christ, of which he said when on earth, " My heart is like wax, it is melted in the midst of my bowels" (Ps. xxii. 14). How intense was the anguish which wrung from him that bitter cry, " My *soul* is exceeding sorrowful, even unto death !" and how tender the love which moved him at the grave of Lazarus, when " He *groaned* in the *spirit* and was troubled !" (Matt. xxvi. 38 ; John xi. 33.)

> " With joy we meditate the grace
> Of our High Priest above;
> His heart is full of tenderness,
> His bowels melt with love."—WATTS.

" His bowels are as bright ivory overlaid with sapphires."   " Of *bright* ivory," that is, of the best sort, as all that is in Christ is. "Overlaid with sapphires"—a stone of a sky-blue colour, so that *the height* and *depth* of the love of Christ, "which passeth knowledge," are at once presented to our view. No wonder if it be found difficult to express it by any earthly comparison—"The experimental knowledge of it will be the best and safest commentary upon it."—DURHAM.

For none has *a heart of love* like Jesus!

Ver. 15. "*His legs are as pillars of marble set upon sockets of fine gold.*"

The word translated "legs" comes from a root, which signifies *to walk*, so that the *ways* or *goings* of the Lord may be understood here. "*All the paths* of the Lord are mercy and truth"—"*All his ways* are judgment" (Ps. xxv. 10; Deut. xxxii. 4). "As the heavens are higher than the earth, so are my ways higher than your ways" (Isa. lv. 8, 9); not "crooked ways," nor uncertain, but "*equal*" (Ezek. xviii. 29), *and sure* "as pillars of marble set upon sockets of fine gold."

It is a source of unspeakable comfort to the believer to be upheld by such Almightiness—"pillars of marble!" The following is a beautiful instance of this:—"I have a very dear boy in my parish," writes the Rev. R. M. M'Cheyne, "who is dying just now. He said to me the other day, 'I have just been feeding for some days on the words you gave me—His legs are as pillars of marble set upon sockets of fine gold; for I am sure he will be able to carry me and all my sins.' "

He is mighty to bear up every believer that is *hung upon him* (Isa. xxii. 23, 24 ; see also Ps. lxxv. 3).

> " Though once he bow'd his feeble knees,
> Loaded with sins and agonies :
> Now on the throne of his command,
> His legs like marble pillars stand."—WATTS.

And the foundation, like the head, is " of fine gold." So divine is Jesus! " The God incarnate, Man divine "—" *Set up* from everlasting, from the beginning," &c. (Prov. viii. 22, 23).

> " *His countenance is as Lebanon, excellent as the cedars.*"

" The word *countenance* is used in Scripture to signify not only the face, but the whole stature of a person, or that which gives one the full sight of all his parts together. Compare 2 Sam. xxiii. 21 (in the original, " a man of countenance ") with 1 Chron. xi. 23. " A man of *stature*."—DURHAM.

It should therefore be, " *His stature* is as Lebanon, excellent as the cedars "—the cedars of Lebanon being unrivalled by any in the world for their loftiness, glory, and majesty ; and, therefore, chosen by the Bride to describe her Beloved. " Excellent," *elect,* or *choice as the cedars.*

And thus she passes from the minor consideration of the several *parts* of his person, in each and all of which he was lovely, to compare him *in his full stature* to the cedars of Lebanon! Truly there is none so glorious, none so " full of majesty," as Jesus !

Ver. 16. *" His mouth is most sweet."*

Literally, " his mouth is sweetness." The *mouth* in this place differs from the *words* of the mouth, or the *lips;* it rather signifies the friendliness or sensible manifestations of the love of Christ, as expressed in chapter i. 2, " Let him kiss me with the kisses of his mouth."—DURHAM.

It is neither hearing him, nor seeing him, *but tasting of his sweetness.* It is as if the Bride had said, Ask ye what my beloved is ? " He is indeed stately to look upon, &c. ; *but,* his mouth, *when it is felt,* in his own kissing of his Bride, by manifestations of his love to her sense—there, there, oh! there, exceeding inexpressible and unconceivable delight and satisfaction is to be found !"—DURHAM.

This was what the Bride knew and enjoyed, of which the daughters of Jerusalem knew nothing. This it is which yields such happiness to believers, to which *professors* are utter strangers. This it is which makes his *absence* so intolerable, and his *presence* so unutterably sweet. " His mouth is sweetness "—sweetness itself, such as no similitude can express. It is but one word in the original, and that in the plural number, signifying the excessive sweetness, the soul-ravishing delight which experimental experiences of the love of Jesus beget in the soul. " Let him kiss me with the kisses of his mouth," for, " his mouth is *most sweet*," yea, " *sweet-nesses !*"

" *Yea, he is altogether lovely.*"

" All over glorious is my Lord."—WATTS.

" He is *all desires*," as it is in the original. It were vain to attempt to say all he is, because there is nothing desirable that is not in him! " In him dwelleth all the fulness of the Godhead bodily!" (Col. i. 19 ; ii. 9.) " All the beauties and perfections that are scattered among creatures are in an eminent and transcendent way gathered together, and to be found in him at once."—DURHAM.

" All my capacious powers can wish
In thee doth richly meet."—DODDRIDGE.

" Join all the glorious names,
Of wisdom, love, and power,
That ever mortals knew,
Or angels ever bore :
All are too mean to speak his worth—
Too mean to set my Saviour forth."—WATTS.

Professors ask, " What is thy beloved more than another beloved ?" The Bride replies, " *Christ is all and in all.*"

" If ask'd what of Jesus I think?
Though still my best thoughts are but poor,
I say, He's my meat and my drink,
My life, and my strength, and my store ;
My shepherd, my husband, my friend,
My Saviour from sin and from thrall,
My hope from beginning to end,
My portion, my Lord, *and my all.*"—NEWTON.

Whom have I need of in heaven but Christ ? and

whom should I desire on earth beside him ? for " *he is all desires.*"

> " *This is my beloved, and this is my friend, O daughters of Jerusalem.*"

This is holy boasting, it is glorying *in the Lord.* This " altogether lovely " one is my Beloved ! Well might she therefore ask, " Is not my beloved more than another beloved, O ye daughters of Jerusalem ?" And the greatest wonder of all is, *He is mine!*—" *my* beloved, *my* friend." Thrice blessed assurance ! " Poor, weak, and worthless though I am, I have a rich, almighty friend," &c. Jesus loves to be thus remembered and spoken of. " They that feared the Lord *spake often* one to another, and the ·Lord *hearkened* and *heard it,*" &c. (Mal. iii. 16). We should think of *his hands and feet* once pierced with nails, but now stretched forth for our salvation ; of *his lips* speaking words of life, peace, and comfort ; of *his bowels* yearning over his dear children ; of *his legs* so mighty to uphold ; and of *his eyes* ever over us for good ! And we should speak of him to others, and be ever telling to sinners around, " What a dear Saviour we have found." Our souls *should* make their *boast* in the Lord, that the humble may hear thereof and be glad (Ps. xxxiv. 2).

But when we remember that this is *our* Beloved, and *our* friend, should not every rising doubt, every anxious fear, every unbelieving thought be silenced ? Is he not able out of the riches of his glory to supply *every need?*   Is he not *always nigh?*—"a God at hand, and not a God afar off"?—"able to do for us exceeding abundantly above all that we ask or think"?   Oh! for more faith, more simple reliance, more abiding confidence in our dear Redeemer! "Perfect love casteth out fear;" and all we want to give us a more unshaken confidence in Jesus, is more of that deep affection and constant love which it is the part of the Bride to exercise towards her Beloved.   We should be so engrossed with the contemplation of the Lord as to forget all meaner things.

> "I travel through a desert drear and wild,
> Yet is my heart with such sweet thoughts beguiled,
> Of HIM on *whom* I lean, my strength, my stay,
> *I can forget* the sorrows of the way."

Such will be more and more the language of our hearts as we are more and more occupied with thoughts "*of him*."   "Jesus Christ, the same yesterday, to-day, and for ever."   "Oh! what a friend is Christ to me!"

> "Our Jesus shall be still our theme,
> While in this world we stay;
> We'll sing our Jesus' lovely name,
> When all things here decay.
>
> "When we appear in yonder cloud,
> With all the ransom'd throng,
> Then will we sing more sweet, more loud,
> And Christ shall be our song."—CENNICK.

"My meditation *of him* shall be sweet."

CHAPTER VI.

The Daughters of Jerusalem.

Ver. 1. " *Whither is thy beloved gone, O thou fairest among women? whither is thy beloved turned aside? that we may seek him with thee.*"

WHAT blessed consequences flow from speaking of Jesus! Not only had the Bride regained her own happy confidence in her Beloved, so that she could say "*this* is my beloved, and *this* is my friend, O daughters of Jerusalem" (chap. v. 16); but *they* have also an earnest desire kindled within them to seek him too! "Whither is thy beloved turned aside? that *we* may seek him with thee." Surely this ought to teach us that, if we would be of use to others, it is *of Jesus* we must speak. He must be the object to which we must direct them, as well as look ourselves; and it is very blessed to be joined in our heavenward way by fresh travellers to Zion, who are attracted thither by our beauty and our joys. We should ever be saying as we go, " Come with us, and we will do thee good ;" and some at least will be induced to seek the Saviour " with " us.

But the believer must also learn from these words how dishonouring his low views of Jesus are. The Bride had said, that "he had withdrawn himself, and was gone ; " and consequently these professors are led to inquire, " Whither he had turned aside ? and whither he was gone ? " as if Jesus ever "turned aside," or ever forsook his people ! It is thus that we cast stumbling-blocks in our brother's way, rendering it difficult for them to know where to find him whom *we* cannot find ! whereas he is ever nigh.

"Say not in thine heart, Who shall ascend into heaven ? (that is, to bring Christ down from above) ; or who shall descend into the deep ? (that is, to bring up Christ again from the dead) ; but what saith it ? the word *is nigh thee*," &c. (Rom. x. 6, &c.)

It is a blessed employment to be "seeking for Jesus " (John vi. 24) ; for he never says, " Seek ye me in vain," but rather, " Seek, *and ye shall find* ; " " Those that seek me early shall find me " (Matt. vii. 7, 8 ; Prov. viii. 17).—For " the Lord is good unto them that wait for him, to the soul that seeketh him," and "is a rewarder of them that diligently seek him " (Lam. iii. 25 ; Heb. xi. 6). " Whither is thy beloved turned aside ? *that we may seek him with thee.*"

THE BRIDE'S REPLY.

Ver. 2. " *My beloved is gone down into his garden, to the beds of spices, to feed in the gardens, and to gather lilies.*"

At once the Bride is able to reply in the confidence of faith, my beloved is in his garden, where he is ever wont to be. It is precious experience; for, whilst speaking to others *of Jesus,* her own sorrows were entirely forgotten. Her thoughts were *turned away from herself,* and all her affections called into exercise towards *him.* And now the eye of faith is fixed upon him, and she *sees* him, and regains her assurance and feels him present! Thus, like Mary, we may often be seeking for Jesus when he is standing beside us, and be speaking to him, though we know it not (John xx. 14, 15). But the moment he is come down *sensibly* into the garden of a believer's soul, that soul immediately cries out, " He is *mine! my* beloved !"

This verse sets forth some of the delightsome occupations of the heavenly husbandman in his garden; he *feeds* there, and he *gathers* his flowers. " My beloved is gone down into his garden, to the beds of spices, *to feed* in the gardens, and *to gather lilies.*" He loves *to reap* the precious fruit of the Spirit sown in each heart: " The husbandman that laboureth must be first partaker of the fruits" (2 Tim. ii. 6). He eats and drinks (chap. v. 1). He sees of the travail of his soul, and is satisfied; *feeding* in his gardens. Oftentimes, indeed, he finds his plants so *choked* with the cares, and riches, and pleasures of this life, that they need purging and pruning; but there are many souls that are as " beds of spices" to the Lord Jesus, and amongst these he goes and feeds.

Again, there are " lilies" growing there, taken

from amongst the thorns, chosen out of the world, and gathered by the Lord to be planted in his garden ; and these he oft-times gathers in a still closer sense to himself, drawing them aside for a season even from their fellow-Christians, by illness or bereavement, to hold near communion with himself. But there is a higher sense still in which he gathers them, namely, when he plucks them out of his garden, to plant them in his own bosom—in the very house and courts of God above. Thus Enoch " was not, for God took him" (Gen. v. 24) ; Jacob was " gathered unto his people" (Gen. xlix. 33) ; Stephen " fell asleep" in Jesus (Acts vii. 60). And so one lily after another *has* been gathered, until there is in heaven already an innumerable multitude of the "Church of the first-born;" and yet lily after lily shall *still* be gathered, until the Saviour comes again and receives us unto himself, sending forth his angels to gather his elect from the four winds, from the one end of heaven to the other, so that *all* shall be safely gathered into the heavenly garner (Matt. xxiv. 31), and be " for ever with the Lord."

Till then we see Jesus "in his garden," nurturing each lily planted there, making it to bud, and blossom, and bring forth fruit, and, when the fruit is *ripe*, immediately putting in the sickle, and placing it in his own bosom (Mark iv. 28, 29, margin). Surely we need not dread to be gathered thus ! We should learn to think of death as the gathering of lilies by the Lord—as going to be *with* " Jesus."

Ver. 3. "*I am my beloved's, and my beloved is mine;
he feedeth among the lilies.*"

The Bride has now recovered through grace the
full assurance of the presence of Jesus in the midst
of her : " He feedeth among the lilies." She has not
a doubt left : " I am my beloved's, and my beloved
is mine." And there is a difference in this expression from a nearly similar one which she had used
before, that may not be without meaning and comfort. For she does not come to this conclusion here
so much from the conviction that Christ is hers *as
that she is Christ's.* She has felt that she cannot give
him up, and may therefore reasonably conclude that
he will not give her up. The two states of mind
are different, and are arrived at through different
stages of experience. In chap. ii. 16, it was the
comparatively young believer drawing the conclusion
that she was the Lord's from the sensible assurance
that he was hers ; but here it is the advanced and
deeply-tried Christian testing the fact that, whether
absent or present, her Beloved was still *her* Beloved,
because she so unfeignedly yielded her whole self to
him—" I am my beloved's." I know it, and therefore I am confident that he also is mine. Like
Thomas, who exclaimed, as soon as ever he beheld
the wounded hands and feet of his Redeemer, " *My*
Lord, and my God !" (John xx. 28); like David,
resting in the calm assurance, " The Lord is *my* shepherd ;" like Mary, boasting herself in the infant
Jesus, " My spirit hath rejoiced in God *my* Saviour ! "

or, like Jeremiah, in the depth of tribulation, declaring, "The Lord is *my* portion, saith my soul, therefore will I hope in him" (Ps. xxiii. 1 ; Luke i. 47 ; Lam. iii. 24). "My beloved is *mine*."

CHRIST.

Ver. 4. "*Thou art beautiful, O my love, as Tirzah.*"

Again the Lord makes mention of the beauty of his Bride! And this without one complaint of her past ingratitude and unkind behaviour towards him. How like Jesus! how divine! how worthy of a God! "He hath not dealt with us after our sins, nor rewarded us according to our iniquities. As far as the east is from the west, so far hath he removed our transgressions from us" (Ps. ciii. 10, 12).

"Thou art beautiful, O my love, as Tirzah." "Tirzah" signifies *pleasing* or *acceptable*; it was the name of the royal palace of the kings of Israel (1 Kings xiv. 17), and was as beautiful as kingly state could make it. The Lord was, therefore, looking upon his Bride, *his Church*, as the royal dwelling-place of the King of kings.

How precious and how wonderful to think of Jesus owning sinners, as "the palace of the King of kings!"—"Beautiful as Tirzah." "So shall *the King* greatly desire *thy beauty*," for he it is that worketh in us the things which are "*well-pleasing* in his sight."

" Comely as Jerusalem."

" Jerusalem " was the residence of the kings of *Judah*, " the place which the Lord chose to put his name there ;" still a royal residence, but in a much higher sense than Tirzah was. So the Lord adds figure to figure, with yet increasing force and significance, to set forth all that his Church was to him. " Comely as Jerusalem."

This is the city whose name shall be " Jehovah-shammah," *the Lord is there* (Ezek. xlviii. 35), " whither the tribes go up, the tribes of the Lord," &c. It is " beautiful for situation, the joy of the whole earth, the city of the great King " (Ps. cxxii. 1, &c. ; Ps. xlviii. 1, &c.) It is surrounded with mountains (Ps. cxxv. 1, 2). encompassed with walls, and bulwarks, and towers (Ps. xlviii. 13), and is " builded as a city that is compact together " (Ps. cxxii. 3). At once setting forth the loveliness, security, unity, and royalty of the Church of Christ, as built upon " the Rock of Ages." And yet the comeliness of the earthly Jerusalem sinks into comparative insignificance with " the heavenly Jerusalem," unto which *we* are come (Heb. xii. 22, and Rev. xxi.)

" Terrible as an army with banners."

The word " terrible " seems to be used here, not so much in the sense of something frightful or awful, as of something *dazzling* and glittering. Just as an army with banners glittering in the sun pre-

K

sents a dazzling spectacle to the natural eye, so the Church of Jesus, clad in the panoply of God, shines with a brilliancy of glory in the eyes of her Beloved. " For the weapons of *our* warfare are *not carnal,* but mighty through God," &c.

We can form no just conception of the sight presented to our Redeemer by his Church militant here on earth, fighting its way through hosts of spiritual enemies, in a world that absolutely lieth *in* the wicked one (1 John v. 19, Gr.) ; every member of that Church bearing in his hand " *the sword* of the Spirit," and taking " *the shield* of faith," &c., and each one fighting under the *banner* of love !—a poor and despised people in the eyes of the world around them, but dazzling and terrible in the sight of Jesus—" as an army with banners." For " we are *more* than conquerors, through him that loved us " (Rom. viii. 37).

> Ver. 5. " *Turn away thine eyes from me, for they have overcome me.*"

What amazing condescension in Jesus, to suffer himself to be " overcome " by his Bride ! Not by carnal weapons, nor by any mightiness of her own, but by the depth of her affections, and intensity of her *love!* " Turn away thine eyes from me, for they have overcome me."

Like Jacob wrestling with the angel, she " had power with God . . . and prevailed " (Gen. xxxii. 28 ; Hos. xii. 4) ; even though the angel had said, " Let me go." And like the disciples journeying to Emmaus, who " constrained " Jesus to go in and abide with them, though he made as though he would have gone further (Luke xxiv. 28, 29). Like Moses, too, whom God forbid to pray, saying, " Let me alone," as though his prayers could prevail with God—and he *did* pray, and *overcame!* (Ex. xxxii. 9-14). For the Lord is under a blessed *necessity* to *yield* to the entreaties of his people, by reason of his own faithful promises. He does not, therefore, intend to check the earnestness of his people in prayer, but designs in this way to provoke and encourage them to still greater importunity ; just as he said before, " Thou hast ravished (or taken away) mine heart with one of thine eyes!" (chap. iv. 9.)

What a blessed result of " looking unto Jesus ! " " Thine eyes have overcome me ! " Alas ! how much we lose by looking at our own hearts instead of " looking *unto Jesus !* " We ought rather to covet the honour and privilege of thus enrapturing his heart—a privilege *which might be ours*, if only we walked " worthy of our high calling."

The expression, " *turn away* thine eyes from me," implies a fixed and steady gaze, such as David's when he said, " Mine eyes are *ever* toward the Lord " (Ps. xxv. 15). We should cultivate this steadfast "looking unto Jesus," that our *eyes* may " *wait* upon the Lord our God " (Ps. cxxiii. 2).

Or the words may be rendered thus :—" Turn thine eyes towards me, for they have lifted me up."

For the Hebrew word, "turn away," signifies also "turn to" (as in 1 Chron. xii. 23) ; and the expression, "they have overcome me," is literally, " they have lifted me up" with strength and comfort (as in Ps. cxxxviii. 3).—ROWBOTHAM.

> " *Thy hair is as a flock of goats that appear from Gilead.*"

God uses no vain repetitions ; there is, therefore, some precious truth to be sought out from the recurrence of this passage from chap iv. 1–3. The Bride had fallen into grievous declension since these words were there uttered. " She might, therefore, think that Christ had other thoughts of her now, and, to remove her suspicion, and shew her that she was the very same to him, he will not only commend her afresh, but in the very same words."—DURHAM.

> Ver. 6, 7. " *Thy teeth are as a flock of sheep which go up from the washing, whereof every one beareth twins, and there is not one barren among them. As a piece of a pomegranate are thy temples within thy locks.*"

" However apt believers may be to slip and fail in their duty, and from their own fickleness to suspect that Christ is changeable also, refusing all past evidences of his love, and the words that have comforted them aforetime. the Lord graciously *repeats what he had said, to prove his unchangeableness.*"— DURHAM.

Our failings and shortcomings, nay, even our backslidings, cannot alter *his* love towards us. "Having loved his own which were in the world, he loved them unto the end" (John xiii. 1). We sadly wrong him and dishonour him when we suspect him of loving us less after a fall, than he did before. It is *limiting* the Holy One of Israel (Ps. lxxviii. 41). Just what the Bride was in chap. iv., before she fell into declension, she is still, in chap. vi., after it.

"His love no variation knows."

And we should adore the gracious condescension of our God in teaching it thus. "Who is a God like unto thee, that pardoneth iniquity, *and passeth by* the transgression of the remnant of his heritage?" (Mic. vii. 18–20.)

> Ver. 8, 9. "*There are threescore queens, and fourscore concubines, and virgins without number. My dove, my undefiled is but one; she is the only one of her mother, she is the choice one of her that bare her.*"

This language is very forcible, if taken as the words of the literal Solomon, to set forth spiritual mysteries. In 1 Kings xi. 3, we read that "he had seven hundred wives, princesses, and three hundred concubines," the strange women whom Solomon loved, "together with (or besides) the daughter of Pharaoh" (1 Kings xi. 1).

But however attractive they may once have appeared to him, he now surveys them, and comparing his Bride with them, he sees how she surpasses them all! And thus he takes occasion to make known the estimation of the Church in the eyes of the Lord Jesus. " My dove, my undefiled is but one;" " Many are called, but few chosen." There are multitudes of professors who call themselves Christians—multitudes with half or divided hearts (fitly represented by concubines or " half-wives "), but it belongs to the Bride alone to be the " dove, the undefiled " of Jesus. " The achath, אַחַת, the one; the yechidah, יְהִיכָה, the darling, the only one; from the root, to be joined—united together."

" But one "—" there is one body, and one Spirit, even as ye are called in one hope of your calling " (Eph. iv. 4). There are " many members," it is true, but it is one and the same Spirit that actuates the whole body.

" The only one of her mother;" such alone as are truly born again of the Spirit can be members of that body. " Baptized into Christ." " No more twain, but one flesh." " There shall be one fold and one shepherd." " That they may be one, even as we are one " (John x. 16 ; xvii. 22).

But it is yet further added, " the choice one of her that bare her;" " chosen in him before the foundation of the world ;" " elect according to the foreknowledge of God the Father," and " chosen to salvation, through sanctification of the Spirit, and belief of the truth" (Eph. i. 4 ; 1 Pet. i. 2 ; 2 Thess. ii. 13).

The Lord Jesus sets his affections on *but one* chosen object. None others share his love with his Bride. " She is the *only* one—the *choice* one ! " the " undefiled ! " " Ye are no more strangers and foreigners," but " very members incorporate into the mystical body of Christ." " *But one.*"

And just as the Bride had boasted of the supreme excellence of her Beloved above every other, saying, " *This* is my beloved, and *this* is my friend," so Christ now compares her with her rival queens, concubines, and virgins, and asserts *her* superiority far above them all, saying, " My dove, my undefiled is but *one*," &c.

> " *The daughters saw her, and blessed her ; yea, the queens and the concubines, and they praised her.*"

" Thy renown went forth among the heathen for thy beauty, for it was perfect through my comeliness which I had put upon thee, saith the Lord" (Ezek. xvi. 14). Such is the beauty of Jesus as reflected in his Church ! Even in the world the Bride is owned as fair, " the fairest among women," and worthy to be " praised." " All that see them shall acknowledge them, that they are the seed which the Lord hath blessed" (Isa. lxi. 9) ; and shall take knowledge of them that they have been with Jesus (Acts iv. 13). But it will be " in the ages to come" that Jesus will be emphatically

" glorified in his saints, and *admired* in all them that believe," even when his perfected Bride " shall *appear* with him in glory," and be no longer *hidden* with Christ in God! It may be that the literal Israel will then discover a meaning in these words, as they gaze upon " the Bride, the Lamb's wife," which cannot be understood in the present dispensation. But it is for us to see, in the language of this book, the mystical and spiritual union existing between the Lord Jesus Christ and every believer composing his true Church.

Oh! to reflect so much of his loveliness as that even strangers may admire his beauty in us!

Ver. 10. " *Who is she that looketh forth as the morning, fair as the moon, clear as the sun, and terrible as an army with banners?*"

It seems as if the Lord would say, And do ye *now* see and admire her beauty? it is but as the early dawn of day. As yet she is but, as it were, emerging from the darkness of the shadow of death; her looking forth is but " as the morning." Ye shall see greater things than these, for she is ordained to shine " more and more *unto the perfect day*" (Prov. iv. 18).

There is great beauty in the two figures here chosen by the Lord as characteristic of his Church — " fair as the moon — clear as the sun." The moon shines, but not with its own light; it is never wholly free from spot or shade, nor does it always

shine with equal light. Fit emblem of the child of
God, as in himself a dark, opaque body, shining *only*
with the *reflected* beams of the Sun of Righteousness—he never reflects that light *perfectly*, nor does
he need to be told how he shines more or less
brightly as he comes nearer or recedes further from
the Sun from whom his light is borrowed. As his
orbit varies, so does his light; yet, in whatever
measure that light shines upon him, he is "*fair*."
" We all beholding as in a glass the glory of the
Lord, are changed into the same image from glory
to glory, even as by the Spirit of the Lord " (2 Cor.
iii. 18).

And just as " the moon " was divinely constituted
" to give light " by night (Gen. i. 15, 16), so does
the Church of Christ shine forth as a light in the
world, all through the present night of darkness,
until the shadows flee away, and she shines forth
" clear as the sun."

" Then shall the righteous shine forth as the sun
in the kingdom of their Father " (Matt. xiii. 43).
From the first moment of her union with Christ,
she is *in him*, " clear as the sun ;" " complete in
him ;" holy as he is holy ; righteous as he is
righteous ; "*perfect*" through the comeliness which
he has put upon her ; for " *as* he is, *so* are we in
this world " (1 John iv. 17). We are one with him
—nay, we are a part of himself—members of his
body, of his flesh, and of his bones. *We* are " made
the righteousness of God in him " (2 Cor. v. 21) ;

" *without spot*," "faultless," "unblameable, and unreprovable;" yea, "*clear* as the sun." Thus (in
Rev. xii. 1) the Church is represented as " a woman
clothed with the sun" (taking the words spiritually); shining forth as one vast constellation of
glory!

Believers cannot see themselves too strongly in
this light—*in Jesus*, justified and sanctified *perfectly*.
For " by him all that believe are justified from all
things," washed, sanctified, and justified, &c. (Acts
xiii. 39; 1 Cor. vi. 11.) Yet in themselves they are
dark as the moon, and ever prone to wax and wane
in holiness. Their *light* depends solely on their
nearness to or distance from " the Sun of Righteousness;" and whilst on the one hand they are
ever variable, ever changing and fluctuating, they
are on the other hand *always* "*clear*," as Jesus is—
clad in *his* righteousness—hidden beneath his body-
covering robe, and *perfect* in his comeliness. " The
glory which thou gavest *me*, I have given *them*,
that they may be one, even as we are one " (John
xvii. 22).

And to all this it is added, that the Church of
Christ is likewise " terrible as an army with banners," *i. e.*, presenting a *dazzling* appearance (see on
ver. 4). It is "fair" and " clear as the sun;" but
it is even more, it is of resplendent brilliancy, of
dazzling brightness! Some commentators even
render the clause, " Dazzling as the streamer" (*i. e.*,
a comet).

Such, then, is the glorious beauty of poor, despised Christians in the sight of Christ !

Ver. 11. "*I went down into the garden of nuts to see the fruits of the valley, and to see whether the vine flourished, and the pomegranates budded.*"

The mention of "the garden *of nuts*" is replete with most precious instruction. The Bride little thought, when she was pursuing her earnest search after Christ, in the former part of the preceding chapter, how that experience was ripening her fruits. She little knew that he was then preparing her for presenting to him these "fruits *of the valley.*" But, oh ! what encouragement it affords for those who are "now *for a season*, if needs be, *in heaviness* through manifold temptations," *for the trial* of their faith ! It is *this* which ripens the autumnal fruits. There had already been the indications of *spring*, so early as the second chapter of the book ;—the passing away of the storms and rain of winter, the flowers appearing on the earth ; the singing of birds, the *green* figs, and the *tender* grape. And there had been, somewhat later, all the lovely evidences of the summer season (in chap. iv.) An orchard of fruit trees, plants, and flowers, and chief spices, and trees of frankincense, all in full perfection ; a garden well watered, and made to emit sweet fragrance through the breathings of the Holy Spirit—"the north wind and the south."

But now another stage of Christian experience

is attained. Jesus finds in the advancing believer a garden *of nuts*, and *"fruits of the valley"*— *autumnal* fruits.

These are not to be found in the young and inexperienced believer, but in the *matured* and *deeply-tried* children of God. Fruits of *humiliation*. Oh! it is well to be brought into the valley of humiliation, for the fruits to be found *there* are carefully looked for, and much valued by our Lord. He who calls himself "the Lily *of the valley*," will not despise "the fruits of the valley" in his people. His eye is ever watching the plants in his garden —he is ever noticing the growth of each (1 John ii. 12–14). "I went down into the garden of nuts, to see the fruits of the valley, and to see whether the vine flourished, and the pomegranates budded." The "*nuts*" and "fruits of *the valley*" represent the fathers in Christ; the *flourishing* vines, the young men; and the *budding* pomegranates, the *babes*. Thus the Lord has his eye upon each; looking for *fruit* in the long-tried Christian, for a *flourishing* state in his vineyard, and in the pome-granates for the *early buds*. "Fruit *in his season*" (Ps. i. 3).

> Ver. 12. "*Or ever I was aware, my soul made me like the chariots of Ammi-nadib*" (margin, "*set me on the chariots of my willing people*," Ps. cx. 3).

This expression seems to denote something of

the same enrapturing feeling on the part of Christ as that in verse 5, "Turn away thine eyes from me, for they have *overcome me;*" or, as in chap. iv. 9, "Thou hast ravished (or taken away) mine heart." The Lord Jesus condescends to be thus acted upon, as it were, by his Bride—the Church.

"Or ever I was aware, my soul set me on the chariots of my willing people"—for so the word "Ammi-nadib" may be rendered. Ammi signifies "my people" (Hosea ii. 1, margin), and Nadib is the word used in Psalm cx. 3, "Thy people shall be *willing,*" &c. The intense earnestness of his Bride for communion with him, the steadfastness with which she looks after him, and the delight with which she welcomes him back, after for a season losing her sensible hold of him, stir up all his inmost affections towards her, so that he is overcome and carried away with them!

What amazing condescension in Jesus, that he should represent himself as *capable* of being so moved by redeemed sinners! Little do we think how, in these ways, we all become the subjects either of *grief* or of *holy delight* to Jesus. Christians do not consider as they ought, the depth and intensity of his feelings towards them. "As the bridegroom rejoiceth over the bride, *so shall thy God rejoice* over thee" (Isa. lxii. 5). Alas! we know but little of sympathy with what he feels—but this should not be in the "members of his body." Should not the hands and feet move at all times in unison with the head? The Lord give us to share more of his joy. (John xv. 11).

It is possible that the ultimate meaning of these words may be in reference to that "moment," when, in the twinkling of an eye, at the last trump, we shall all be changed, and Jesus shall see of the travail of his soul and shall be satisfied—when he will, as it were, forget the anguish of his travail, in the joy of the perfect manifestation of the sons of God.

Of that moment alone could it be said, in the full sense of the words, "Or ever I was aware," or, "*I knew not:*" but "of that day and hour knoweth no man : no, not the angels which are in heaven, neither the Son, but the Father" (Mark xiii. 32).

But it will be when the autumnal fruits of the Church are fully ripe that the sickle will be put in, "because the harvest is come" (Mark iv. 28, 29, margin). The Lord Jesus will be in his garden inspecting the fruits, when he shall be, as it were, transported or carried away "on the chariots of his willing people;" and so shall they "ever be with the Lord." "In a moment, in the twinkling of an eye."—"Or ever I was aware."

THE DAUGHTERS OF JERUSALEM.

Ver. 13. "*Return, return, O Shulamite; return, return, that we may look upon thee.*"

The Lord has represented himself as carried away with his Bride, and this excites the cry from the daughters of Jerusalem, "Return, return, that we may look upon thee." Just as in 2 Sam. xix. 14, "All the men of Judah sent this word unto the king, *Return, thou and all thy servants.*" And whether the words be taken in reference to the whole Church, as caught up to meet the Lord in the air, or only to each individual member, as caught away in death, it is equally impossible for those who are left behind to follow them.

> "In vain my fancy strives to paint
> The moment after death," &c.

They can but long for *the manifested glory* of Christ and his Bride, at his coming again. Then each lost one will be found again ; then Jesus will be "*admired*" in and by them (2 Thess. i. 10). Then the daughters, the queens, and the concubines will at once see, and bless, and praise "the Bride— the Lamb's wife ;" and in looking at each glorified believer, they will but be looking *at Jesus.* "Return, return, that we may look upon *thee.*"

For then, if it be asked—

"*What will ye see in the Shulamite?*"

The answer will be at once given—

"*As it were the company of two armies.*"

Jesus and his Bride are emphatically one ! This is "the great mystery" of this blessed book. They are no longer twain, but one!—for Christians are taken *into Christ*, and their life, which is now "*hid* with Christ in God," shall then be *revealed* with him in glory.

Oh! what a wonderful position he has brought us into! Co-kings with Jesus, and even more—for we are "*the Lamb's wife*," the spouse of the Son of God—taken into marriage union with him, and entering with him *into God!* "That they may be ONE, as we are." "Two armies" might be rendered "two hosts" (compare Gen. xxxii. 2). *Two, in one.* How sweet to be thus in "the company" of Jesus, and to be seen "IN" him!

"*In* the Shulamite" shall be seen "as it were the company of Mahanaim," or *two* hosts (margin). "As thou, Father, art in me, and I in thee, that they also may be one in us" (John xvii. 21, 22).

CHAPTER VII.

THE DAUGHTERS OF JERUSALEM.

Ver. 1. "*How beautiful are thy feet with shoes, O prince's daughter!*"

THERE is a change in the form of address in these words—from a bride to a "prince's *daughter*"—rendering it probable that here the daughters of Jerusalem *are looking* at the Bride "in the Shulamite," according to their desire (chap. vi. 13). They see in her the daughter of the King of kings, the everlasting Father, given to his Son as "the Bride, the Lamb's wife." They own her royalty ; they admire her beauty. "The King's daughter is all glorious within," &c. (Ps. xlv. 10–15). "How beautiful are thy feet with shoes, O prince's daughter !" "Behold what manner of love *the Father* hath bestowed upon us, that we should be called *the sons* of God !" (1 John iii. 1.) "Ye shall be *my sons and daughters*, saith the Lord Almighty" (2 Cor. vi. 18).

What a precious word it was that was spoken by the Lord Jesus, when on earth, to the poor woman who came behind him trembling, "*Daughter*, be of good comfort!" &c. (Luke viii. 48). How wonderful to be owned in such a relation! and how we ought to glory in such a relationship! For what does not the charter of adoption into God's family include? what are not the children of the Most High God entitled to? "If children, then heirs; *heirs of God*, and *joint heirs with Christ!*" —They shall "*inherit all* things"—"All are yours, and ye are Christ's, and Christ is God's"—"Son, thou art ever with me, and all that I have is thine" (Rom. viii. 17; Rev. xxi. 7; 1 Cor. iii. 22, 23; Luke xv. 31).

"It is your Father's good pleasure to give you the kingdom," "O prince's daughter!" for he "hath called you unto his kingdom and glory" (Luke xii. 32; 1 Thess. ii. 12).

The Bride is now surveyed from head to foot. In chapters iv. and vi. only *parts* of her person were noticed; but she has now advanced to great maturity of Christian experience, even to perfection, to "the measure of the stature of the fulness of Christ." Her stature, from the soles of her feet to the crown of her head, "is like unto a palm-tree." Oh! what a marvellous change for beggars from the dunghill, where, "from the sole of the foot even unto the head," we were as a mass of "wounds and bruises, and putrifying sores" (Isa. i. 6), to be set among princes, and made to inherit the throne of glory! (1 Sam. ii. 8.) How it magnifies "the ex-

ceeding riches of his grace in his kindness toward
us through Christ Jesus !"

"How beautiful are thy feet with shoes!"—"Your
feet shod with the preparation of the gospel of peace"
(Eph. vi. 15). But the word translated "feet" is
more correctly rendered "footsteps," referring rather
to the ways and goings of the children of God. "The
steps of a good man are ordered by the Lord," &c.—
"To guide our feet into the way of peace"—"Thy
word is a lamp unto my feet, and a light unto my
path" (Ps. xxxvii. 23 ; Luke i. 79 ; Ps. cxix. 105).

"Thou shalt *remember all the way* which the Lord
thy God led thee these forty years," &c. (Deut. viii.
2). And Jesus is "the way" in whom *we* have to
walk. "As ye have therefore received Christ Jesus
the Lord, so *walk ye in him*" (Col. ii. 6). While
Moses was commanded to *put off his shoes*, because the
place whereon he stood was holy ground (Exod. iii.),
we are invited to draw near *with boldness*, in full assurance of faith, by "a new *and living way*"—even
Jesus (Heb. x. 19, &c. ; John xiv. 6). Oh ! to
"walk worthy of the Lord unto all pleasing !" Well
may we pray with David, "Hold up my goings in
thy paths, that my footsteps slip not" (Ps. xvii. 5).

> "*The joints of thy thighs are like jewels, the work of
> the hands of a cunning workman.*"

Such is the beautiful symmetry of the Church of
Christ !—"The whole body *fitly joined together*, and
compacted by that *which every joint* supplieth"—

" The head, from which all the body by *joints and
bands* having nourishment ministered, increaseth
with the increase of God" (Eph. iv. 13–16 ; Col. ii.
19). " Your loins girt about with truth" (Eph. vi.
14). " Wherefore gird up the loins of your mind"
—"Your loins girded" (1 Pet. i. 13 ; Luke xii. 35).
" The *joints* of thy thighs are like jewels."

Nor are we to forget the Divine Architect of the
body so fearfully and wonderfully made (compare
Ps. cxxxix. 14–16, with Eph. v. 29, 30, 32). All is
" the work of the hands of a cunning workman."
" Ye also are builded together for an habitation of
God *through the Spirit*" (Eph. ii. 22).

For as the typical tabernacle could not be reared
until God had filled Bezaleel " *with the Spirit of God,
in wisdom, and in knowledge, and in all manner of
workmanship to devise cunning works*," &c. (Exod.
xxxi. 1–5), so it is said of the Lord Jesus, " the
Spirit of the Lord shall rest upon him, the spirit of
wisdom and understanding, the spirit of counsel and
might, the spirit of knowledge and of the fear of the
Lord ; and shall make him *of quick understanding*,"
&c. (Isa. xi. 2, 3). For he is the potter who hath
power over the clay, to fashion it into vessels of
glory, whereby he may " *make known* the riches
of his glory " (Rom. ix. 21, 23).

Ver. 2. " *Thy navel is like a round goblet, which
wanteth not liquor ; thy belly is like an heap of
wheat set about with lilies.*"

The chief thought suggested by these expressions is that of great abundance : " A round goblet which *wanteth not liquor, and an heap* of wheat set about with lilies." " Bread shall be given him, his waters shall be sure " (Isa. xxxiii. 16).

This is the promised inheritance of the people of the Lord—" a land of brooks of *water*, of *fountains*, and *depths*, that spring out of valleys and hills ; a land of *wheat* and *barley*—a land of oil olive, and honey—a land wherein thou shalt *eat bread without scarceness*, thou shalt *not lack anything* in it" (Deut. viii. 7-9). Truly indeed, in our " Father's house there is *bread enough* and to spare."

" He should have fed them also with the finest of the wheat" (Ps. lxxxi. 16 ; cxlvii. 14 ; Mat. v. 6 ; Jer. xxxi. 14, &c. &c.)

" O fear the Lord, ye his saints, for there is *no want* to them that fear him. They that seek the Lord *shall not want any good thing*" (Ps. xxxiv. 9, 10).

No wonder, therefore, that the language of the Bride should be, " My cup *runneth over*" (Ps. xxiii. 5). She is " satisfied with favour, and *full* with the blessing of the Lord " (Deut. xxxiii. 23)—" *Filled* with comfort "—" *Filled* with the Spirit "—*Filled* " with all joy and peace in believing "—" *Full* of goodness, *filled* with all knowledge "—Yea, " *Filled* with *all the fulness of God*" (2 Cor. vii. 4 ; Eph. v. 18 ; Rom. xv. 13, 14 ; Eph. iii. 19).

Ver. 3. " *Thy two breasts are like two young roes that are twins.*"

The children of one family—" Be ye all of one mind, having compassion one of another : *love as brethren* "—" That there be no divisions among you, but that ye be *perfectly joined together* in the same mind, and in the same judgment," even as twins of one size and age (1 Pet. iii. 8 ; 1 Cor. i. 10). Such should ever be the *unity* of the Church of Christ, for she is, in the figurative language of Scripture, "the mother of us all." And, as if to intimate that in the heavenly family there is no difference made between the elder and the younger children, they are represented as " twins," heirs alike of God, and joint heirs with Christ.

Ver. 4. " *Thy neck is as a tower of ivory.*"

Ivory is in itself exceeding costly and precious, so that a tower of it bespeaks a degree of exaltation of no ordinary kind. Truly Christians have *a high* and holy calling, and are raised to an extraordinary altitude of glory, displaying the riches of the King of kings, and making known "*what* is the hope of his calling, and what the riches of the glory of his inheritance in the saints" (Eph. i. 18).

We read that King Solomon made himself a throne of ivory (2 Chron. ix. 17), but " the greater than Solomon," in the exceeding riches of his grace, does more than this, for he raises his Bride *to share his throne* (Rev. iii. 21). Believers may learn from this figure something of the *exalted position* they are destined to fill in glory—" thy neck is as a tower of ivory."

" *Thine eyes like the fish-pools in Heshbon, by the gate of Bath-rabbim.*"

The import of this figure seems to be the setting forth of clearness and transparency of character— " If thine *eye* be *single*, thy whole body shall be full of light " (Matt. vi. 22). There must be a holy sincerity about God's people — no darkness, but transparent clearness—" *light* in the Lord " (Eph. v. 8). This is a point much dwelt upon in the heavenly Jerusalem, the figurative representation of " the Bride the Lamb's wife "—" her *light* was like unto a stone most precious . . *clear* as crystal." " And the city was *pure gold*, like unto *clear glass*, and as it were *transparent* glass " (Rev. xxi. 9–11, 18, 21 ; see also Rev. iv. 6). " And before the throne there was *a sea of glass* like unto crystal." We should therefore seek to be " *sincere* and without offence," *cleansed* from all filthiness of the flesh and spirit, " *sprinkled* from an evil conscience—*washed* with pure water," doing the will of our God, not with eye-service, " but in *singleness* of heart " (Phil. i. 10 ; 2 Cor. vii. 1 ; Heb. x. 22). " Mine eyes are ever toward the Lord " (Ps. xxv. 15).

" *Thy nose is as the tower of Lebanon, which looketh toward Damascus.*"

From a tower situated on the heights of Lebanon the eye would readily survey the surrounding country in the plains below ; and it is scarcely possible to conceive a figure more strikingly calculated to represent the state of mind which has been so beautifully described as the true character of the Christian's walk, " not looking up from earth to heaven, but down from heaven to earth."

And if (as is commonly supposed) Damascus is mentioned as the enemies' land, our duty is plainly pointed out as exercising habitual, constant watchfulness against our spiritual enemies—" Thy nose is as the tower of Lebanon, which looketh toward Damascus."

The watchman must be ever on the alert to give the alarm on the first appearance of the enemy, and the Christian must be ready to wage perpetual war against the first risings of the flesh, the world, or the devil.

Ver. 5. " *Thine head upon thee is like Carmel, and the hair of thine head like purple.*"

The word " Carmel " is rendered " crimson " in the margin ; and, if this be the correct translation, the idea suggested would be that of *royalty*, of which purple and crimson were the ordinary representatives. The Church of Christ is, therefore, set forth as the Bride of the King of kings—sharing his throne, and reigning with him. This is her purchased privilege. He hath " made us unto our God

kings and priests," and we shall " reign on the earth "
(Rev. i. 6, and v. 10), even " for ever and ever "
(Rev. xxii. 5).

But if *Carmel* be intended, the idea is rather that
of richness, fertility, and profusion (see Isa. xxxv.
2 ; Mic. vii. 14). In either case, the magnificence
and exceeding excellence of this " glorious Church "
is displayed ; and our earnest care, as individual
members of it, ought to be to bear fruit in this rich
profusion—not thirty-fold only, nor sixty-fold, but
a hundred-fold !

" *The king is held in the galleries.*"

The royal Bride detains the King, and will not
let him go. He is bound to dwell in his house,
" whose house are *we*." The word " galleries " is
the same with that in chap. ii. 17, " *the rafters* "—
" The beams of our house are cedar, and *the rafters*
of fir." For " the tabernacle of God is with men,
and he will *dwell* with them " (Rev. xxi. 3).
Throughout eternity the King will be bound in the
galleries of his Church, just as he is now under a
blessed constraint to abide with us, because he has
said, " I will never leave thee." He cannot leave
his Bride, for they are one. He dwells in the midst
of us, and *in* each one of us, making sinners' hearts
his royal palace !

Oh ! what a cluster of privileges is here grouped
together as belonging to the children of God's royal
family (the " prince's daughter "), and all coming to

them as reclaimed prodigals returning to their Father's house !

They are, *first,* clothed with " the best robe," the marriage " ring " is placed on their hand, " *and shoes* on their *feet* " (Luke xv. 22). " How beautiful are thy feet with shoes !"

Second, They are all " fitly framed and joined together," speaking oftentimes one to another, that they may be the Lord's in the day when he *makes up his jewels* (Mal. iii. 16, 17). " The joints of thy thighs are like jewels."

Third, They find abundance of the best provisions —" bread enough and to spare." They are continually feasting by faith upon the body broken and the blood shed, which is " *meat indeed, and drink indeed* " (compare John vi. 55 with ver 2). " A *heap* of wheat—a round goblet that wanteth not liquor."

Fourth, They are all alike the children of one Father, the heirs of the same inheritance—their hearts being " *knit together* in love," in strong family affection, and " unity of spirit "—having " one Lord, one faith," " one God and Father." " *As twins.*"

Fifth, They are raised to an exceeding height of glory—pressing toward the mark for the prize of their *high* calling in Christ Jesus. Their hearts being continually called " thither to ascend, where their Saviour, Christ, is gone before," and their affections being set " on things *above,* and not on things on the earth" (Col. iii. 1, 2). "Thy neck is as a tower of ivory."

Sixth, There is a lovely *reflection* of the *Father's image* in them; even "*as in water* face *answereth to face!*" "Beholding as in a glass the glory of the Lord, are changed into the same image" (2 Cor. iii. 18), and become holy as he is holy, purifying themselves even as he is pure, knowing that soon they will be perfectly like him, for they will "see him as he is." But even *now* they are the sons of God (1 John iii. 1–3)—"*children* of *light,*" full of holy transparency and sincerity. "Thine eyes like the fishpools," &c.

Seventh, They set themselves, like Habakkuk, on their "watch-tower," jealously to guard the approach of every enemy, and diligently obeying their Lord's command to "*watch*" (Mark xiii. 37; Hab. ii. 1)— looking down upon earthly things, whilst their conversation, their citizenship, is *in heaven.* "Thy nose is as the tower of Lebanon," &c. (ver. 4).

Eighth, They "bring forth much fruit" to the glory of God, so that he compares them to "the excellency of *Carmel*" (Isa. xxxv. 2)—not content with low and ordinary attainments, but clothed in royal apparel, in purple and crimson, as became a "prince's daughter" (ver. 5).

Oh to "walk worthy" of this our regal station! Then our footsteps would indeed be "beautiful;" for our walk would be *God's walk in us,* as it is written, "I will dwell in them, and *walk* in them."

The King walking in the galleries of his Church, is held therein.

Ver. 6. *" How fair and how pleasant art thou, O love, for delights!"*

No wonder, after such a view of the Bride of Christ, that the daughters of Jerusalem should exclaim how fair and pleasant she appeared. They have surveyed her from head to foot, and her whole person is commended by them—" Thy feet, thy thighs, thy navel, thy belly, thy two breasts, thy neck, thine eyes, thy nose, thy head," yea, even " the *hair* of thine head " (or, as the word is in the original, " *the smallest thing* "). All, from the least to the greatest, set forth her beauty. And thus the Church of Christ, the Bride of Jesus, displays the marvellous skill of the " cunning workman," so fearfully and wonderfully is she made, and so " curiously wrought" (Ps. cxxxix. 14–16). " Thine eyes did see my substance, yet being imperfect ; and in thy book all my members were written, *which in continuance were fashioned,* when as yet there was none of them." " The work of the hands of a cunning workman."

But if each believer, as he ripens for heaven, becomes individually an object of admiration and delight to Jesus, how much more will the perfected body in glory shew forth his praise ! Then not one member will be wanting, but *all* shall have been " fashioned," and the stature of the " *perfect* man " attained. *Every* member will be there, down to the humblest and feeblest lamb in Christ's fold. Yea, from the feet to the head, from the lowest member, gradually mounting up to the highest, " *every one of them* " is *set in the body* as it hath pleased God (1 Cor. xii. 18, &c.) " How fair and how pleasant art thou, O love, for delights ! "

Jehovah rejoiced, in like manner, over the works of creation, as he successively beheld each day's work, and saw that it was " very good ; " and when at length the six days' work was ended, he looked down from heaven and " saw *everything* that he had made, and behold it was very good" (Gen. i. 31). And shall not the joy of the new creation, the perfecting of the saints, the ending of the six thousand years' patient labour of the Heavenly Husbandman, yield him yet greater delight ? For when the sinners are consumed out of the earth, and the millennial Sabbath shall commence, *then* " the glory of the Lord shall endure for ever ; the Lord shall *rejoice in his works* " (Ps. civ. 30, 31). Then it shall be said to the earthly Jerusalem, " He will rejoice over thee with joy ; he will rest in his love ; he will joy over thee with singing ;" and " Ye shall be a *delightsome* land ! " (Zeph. iii. 17 ; Mal. iii. 12). And to the heavenly Jerusalem, " how fair and how pleasant art *thou*, O love, for delights ! " (Rev. xxi. 9, &c.)

Ver. 7. " *This thy stature is like to a palm-tree, and thy breasts to clusters of grapes.*"

"The righteous shall flourish like the palm-tree"
(Ps. xcii. 12). "The ivy creeps, and the bramble
trails, but the palm, in perpendicular uprightness,
dwells on high, and seeks the things above. . . . .
Some trees are crooked, but the palm is straight;
and, standing forth in its unbending altitude, it
spreads all its foliage to the sun. . . . . It is not
only erect and tall, its stem is fair and even. It is
a tree of remarkable beauty. Apart from all its associations, there is something in its slim uprightness,
its verdant canopy, and the silvery flashes of its
waving plumes, which glads the eye that gazes."

Such is the tree to which the Church of Christ
is likened. "This thy stature is like to a palm-
tree "—tall, erect, and fruitful. But which of us
has attained to it ? Let us forget the things which
are behind, and be ever *reaching forth* unto those
things which are before—pressing toward the mark
of our *high* calling. Let us leave the low and
stunted attainments of those who are but laying
again the foundations of the principles of the doc-
trines of Christ, and let us " go on *unto perfection* "
(Heb. vi. 1).

"Let us lay aside every weight, and the sin
which doth so easily beset us, and let us run with
patience the race that is set before us, looking *unto
Jesus*," for we should be contented with no lesser
standard. He *has* run *his* race, and "is set down at
the right hand of the throne of God" (Heb. xii. 1,
2), a beautiful example for us to follow !

The palm-tree is constantly referred to in Scripture as the emblem *of victory* (see Lev. xxiii. 40 ; John xii. 13 ; and Rev. vii. 9). The saints in glory, who are set down with Jesus *in his throne* (Rev. iii. 21, and iv. 6), are "clothed with white robes, and *palms* in their hands." *Then,* emphatically, it will be true of us, that "we are *more than conquerors* through him that loved us" (Rom. viii. 37).

Nor is this all ; for it is added, "and thy breasts like clusters of grapes." "I am the vine, ye are the branches." All the "fruits of righteousness are by Jesus Christ," &c. (Phil. i. 11). Every bough, therefore, should be bringing forth fruit by abiding in him ; and in "*clusters,*" not sparingly, that our heavenly Father may be glorified (John xv. 1–8.) *By our fruits* we shall be known : for grapes cannot be gathered of thorns—a corrupt tree cannot bring forth good fruit (Matt. vii. 16–20). If there be, therefore, "clusters of grapes" in any believer, it proves him to be grafted into Christ.

> Ver. 8. "*I said, I will go up to the palm-tree, I will take hold of the boughs thereof; now also thy breasts shall be as clusters of the vine, and the smell of thy nose like apples.*"

The daughters of Jerusalem are no longer content to gaze upon the Bride of Jesus, as it were at a distance : "I will *go up* to the palm-tree, I will *take hold* of the boughs thereof." Exalted as she is, and high as is her stature, they resolve to "go up" and

" take hold " of her.   There is something very forcible in this language, for the branches of the palm
grow near the top of the tree, leaving the stem bare
for a considerable height ; so that to " take hold of
the boughs thereof" implies the determination to
press towards the mark of her high calling.   It was
a blessed resolution ; and the result of the communion thus enjoyed was very sweet and refreshing.
" Now also thy breasts shall be as clusters of the
vine."   " That ye may suck and be satisfied with
the breasts of *her consolations* . . . and be delighted
with the abundance of her glory" (Isa. lxvi. 11).
We are beautifully reminded from whom her fruit
is found (Hos. xiv. 8), " Clusters *of the vine*," for
grapes derive all their sweetness *from the vine,* and
Jesus says, " I am the true vine."   Whatever the
Church has, she has in virtue of her union with the
Lord Jesus Christ, her " beloved."

" And the smell of thy nose like apples ; " like
the fruit of that " apple-tree" to which Christ was
likened in chapter ii. 3.   There should be a holy
fragrance around the children of God, that all may
take knowledge of them that they have been *with
Jesus* (Acts iv. 13).

> Ver. 9. " *And the roof of thy mouth like the best
> wine for my beloved, that goeth down sweetly,
> causing the lips of those that are asleep to speak.*"

Such should be the vivifying, refreshing, and
quickening influence of the words uttered by every

child of God — quickening to those who are "*dead in trespasses and sins;*" and reviving to such of the Lord's people as are in a dull, languishing, slumbering state. Words spoken *for his sake*, are words spoken for him, which he takes as *to himself,* and they are sweet to him. If, then, "a cup of cold water" given to one of his little ones in his name, is so graciously owned and accepted of him (Matt. x. 42), how much more "*the best wine!*"

"The best wine" *may* have some future allusion to the feast in the kingdom, of which the Lord has said, "I will drink no more of the fruit of the vine, until that day that I drink it *new* in the kingdom of God" (Mark xiv. 25). But of those times very little is revealed to us in Scripture—"the day shall declare it." In the meantime, it is for us to seek the simple, practical, spiritual meaning of the words; and deeply humbling indeed it is to understand them *so* little, and to have attained to *so very little* of "the measure of the stature of the fulness of Christ!"

THE BRIDE.

Ver. 10. "*I am my beloved's, and his desire is toward me.*"

The Bride is now heard to speak again, but it is in that *advanced stage* of Christian experience, which looks not so much at her own things, as at *the things*

M

of others. There is a very evident difference discernible in her experience onwards to the end of the book. The spring, the summer, and the autumnal seasons have been passed through, and we have now the matured and ripened believer brought before us, full of earnest desire for the good of others.

" I am my beloved's, and his desire is toward me." This is the language of strong, unhesitating confidence in God ; the well-assured, deliberate conviction of the mind. It is most blessed experience to *know* ourselves thus to be the Lord's ; and it is a lesson to be *learnt,* through " manifold temptations for the trial of our faith " (such, for instance, as the Bride had gone through in chapters iii. and v. of this book). But when we are tried we shall come forth as gold, " in *full assurance* of faith," " *nothing wavering :*" able to say with David, " I am thy servant "—" O Lord, truly *I am* thy servant "—" *I am thine;* save me " (Ps. cxix. 94, 125 ; Ps. cxvi. 16).

This full assurance becomes to the child of God the same sure ground for expecting safety and divine keeping, as it was to God's well-beloved Son, when, in pleading with his Father in behalf of his people, he urges this plea—" I pray for them, ... FOR they are *thine* " (John xvii. 9). " I am my beloved's."

There is something very sweet in the feeling that we are the *property* and *possession* of Jesus—" my beloved's "—his own " purchased possession " (Eph. i. 14). Ye are not your own, for ye are *bought* with a price ; therefore glorify God in your body and in your spirit *which are God's*" (1 Cor. vi. 19, 20). Body, soul, and spirit, *all* are *his!* " I," that is, *I myself,* " am my beloved's :" all I have, and all I am —his purchased property. " Whether we live, therefore, or die, we are *the Lord's*" (Rom. xiv. 7, 8).

Nor is this all ; for there is, on the other hand, no doubting of Christ's affection in return ; " and *his* desire is *toward me.*" " Perfect love casteth out fear," and in the exercise of ardent love towards her Beloved, the Bride rested in the full assurance of his love to her. He had given *the strongest* proof of it, in that he had laid down his *life* for her ! And over and over again he had manifested the yearning " desire" of his heart towards her. On one occasion he declared that he was " *straitened*" until baptized with the baptism of death for his people (Luke xii. 50) : on another, he *wept* over Jerusalem, with the " desire" he felt for its salvation (Luke xix. 41, 42 ; Matt. xxiii. 37) : his bowels *yearned* over Ephraim, when he heard him bemoaning himself, &c. (Jer. xxxi. 20) : to his disciples at the last passover, he expressed himself with the deepest intensity of feeling, saying, " *With desire* I have *desired* to eat this passover with you before I suffer ;" or, as it is in the margin, " I have *heartily desired*" (Luke xxii. 15) : and in his last prayer he seems, as it were, to sum up *all* his *desires* for his people, saying to his Father, " I *pray* for them," &c. &c. ; until at length he almost *ceases* to *pray* as a suppliant, saying, " Father, I WILL," &c. (John xvii.)

So earnest was he in our behalf! Nor is this all; he even lives to make intercession for us still— (Heb. vii. 25)—ever breathing out his *desires* in behalf of his Church into his Father's ear, "*until* the shadows flee away" and the day come, when the whole being perfected in glory, " he shall see of the travail of his soul, and shall be *satisfied*."

" So shall the King *greatly desire* thy beauty." " All the invitations of the gospel may be regarded as *the desires* of the heavenly suitor."—MRS STEVENS.

There is yet much comfort to be derived from the *personal appropriation* of these truths, as here expressed. "*I* am my beloved's, and his desire is toward *me:*" each individual member is to realise this for himself. If Christ loves the flock, he loves *every sheep.* " What man, having an hundred sheep, if he lose *one,* doth not . . . go after *that* which is lost?" &c. (Luke xv. 4, &c.) " His desire is towards *me.*" " Who loved *me,* and gave himself for *me*" (Gal. ii. 20).

Such is the happy and assured confidence of the well-established Christian. He is not like " a wave of the sea driven with the wind and tossed" (Jas. i. 6), for *he knows* whom he has believed (2 Tim. i. 12), even " Jesus Christ, the same yesterday, and to-day, and for ever."

The verse may be rendered, " I am my beloved's, because his affection is toward me."—ROWBOTHAM.

Ver. 11. " *Come, my beloved, let us go forth into the field, let us lodge in the villages.*"

The Bride has learnt now to forsake the company of the nearest and dearest, for the sake of Jesus. " Let us go forth into the fields," is the breathing of her soul into the ear of Jesus, expressive of the deep longing she felt for that deep, and close, and intimate communion which could be realised only in retirement.

She would therefore " go forth"—she would leave " the city," the public ordinances, the busy, active scenes of daily life, and the society of the dearest earthly friends, and with her Beloved alone she would " go forth into the fields."

There is great blessedness in being thus for a season *alone with Jesus.* The Lord himself was wont, when on earth, to withdraw with his disciples from the multitude at certain seasons, as in Mark vi. 31, " Come ye yourselves apart into a desert place, and rest a while." He does not say, Go and live in the desert, separate yourselves altogether from your fellow-creatures, and abide in seclusion. God forbid ! He would have them as *lights in the world,* as *messengers* to prepare his way before him, as *witnesses* of his truth in the midst of an ungodly generation.

But, in order to shine brightly, the lamp must be *trimmed;* in order to catch men, the nets must be *mended;* and, in order to teach others, *we must be taught.* Nay, more, for, in order to our *own* growth in grace, and our *own* personal preparation for the presence of the Lord, we need much secret discipline, much secret intercourse with our Father which seeth in secret, and much secret communion with the Beloved of our souls. Hence the manifold means made use of for our withdrawment from this vain, transitory world, from time to time. Too often, alas! the child of God is apt to murmur and repine on being withdrawn from active service and the public ordinances (it may be by illness, &c. &c.), to be taught of Jesus in secret; but the Bride had attained to more of the mind of Christ; for she herself desires it. She would not make it necessary (if one may so speak) that the Lord should lay his chastening hand upon her, to bring her there; but her own soul sighs for this close communion with him.

Those who have once tasted of its sweetness will oftentimes be willing to forego the society of all other beloveds, for that of *the* Beloved—the one, the only one, who can enter into the very inmost recesses of the heart. If we are very closely united to Jesus, we shall pant after this secret intimacy, which is not to be enjoyed in the society even of fellow-Christians. " Come, my beloved, let us go forth into the field."

But the expression that follows intimates the *temporary* nature of this sweet enjoyment: " let us *lodge* in the villages." " For here we have no continuing city;" we are but strangers and pilgrims, tarrying or lodging for the night.

We have a beautiful instance of precisely similar feeling in our Lord when on earth (for the *same Spirit* dwelt in him and actuated him then, which now dwells in and actuates his Bride), leading him to withdraw from the busy city, and lodge in the quiet village. For we read, that after his public entrance into Jerusalem and his ministrations in the temple, " he left them, and went *out of* the *city*, into Bethany ; *and he lodged there*" (Matt. xxi. 17); there, in quiet, peaceful retirement, to hold communion with the family whom he loved (John xi. 1, 5).

The word translated " lodge " may also be rendered to *remain* or continue. But in either case the intent of the passage is, that the Bride longed to be retired from the trouble and distractions of the flesh, and to walk into the field of heavenly meditation and delight.

> Ver. 12. *" Let us get up early to the vineyards ; let us see if the vine flourish, whether the tender grape appear, and the pomegranates bud forth."*

It was not to indulge in carnal ease or sensual enjoyment that the Bride had sought retirement with Jesus. On the contrary, that season of communion was the means of *quickening* her to renewed earnestness and more diligent watchfulness—" Let us *get up early* to the vineyards." " While we have time, let us do good unto all men." " Work while it is called to-day." Like our blessed Saviour, let us learn to rise up early in the morning, " a great while before day " (Mark i. 35). " Let us get up *early* to the vineyards."

And let us remember to go to no work alone, without Jesus—" let *us* go." Never let us go to inspect the vineyards save in company with him.

" To the vineyards." This is just as it should be ; there is first a holy concern for her own well-being, and then afterwards for the welfare of *others* (see chap. viii.) She would look to her own state before God. " Let us *see* if the vine flourish," &c. This intimates diligence and watchfulness. " Look to yourselves that we lose not those things which we have wrought" (2 John 8). " Give *diligence* to make your calling and election sure ;" " for if these things be in you and abound, they make you that ye shall neither be barren nor unfruitful," &c. (2 Pet. i. 8, 10 ; margin, " *idle*"). The contrast is very precious from the present experience of the Bride to her early experience, in chap. i. 6. *Then* she confessed—" but mine own vineyard have I not kept." Now she can get up early to see that the vine is *flourishing*, and the grape *opening* (margin). Thus there is real growth in grace manifested in her. There is likewise a beautiful *reflection* of the Spirit of Jesus in her. Precisely what he had *gone down* into his garden to do (chap. vi. 11), she would now "*get up early* to the vineyards " to do.

But it is observable that the evidences here sought after are not to prove that she is in Christ ;

they are for the *fruits* which are to be found in
Christians. The Bride looks for fruitfulness " in
the *vineyards*," not in the barren wilderness. There
cannot be such fruits in the soul but newly con-
verted : they are only to be found in the trees that
have been digged about (Luke xiii. 8), and in the
branches that have been pruned and purged (John
xv. 2). This is a truth of great importance, though
but seldom thought of. And hence the young believer is oftentimes led to great questionings whether
he is a believer or not, although the question of
fruitfulness scarcely belongs to *him*. How vain for a
soul to be seeking " the tender grape," when it has no
assurance of being a branch of " the vine!" No—it
is when we are brought to say, " I am my beloved's,"
&c., that it becomes us to see that such a *profession*
stands the test of *bearing fruit!* (Matt vii. 17.)

" *There will I give thee my loves.*"

" There "—that is, in the free and unfettered
communion which the Bride enjoyed with Jesus in
solitude would be the *open manifestation* of the
overflowings of her love, which was in measure kept
in restraint in the presence of others. Just as
Joseph, in the intensity of *his* love towards his
brethren, sought his chamber where he might weep
unseen, so it is *in retirement* that we can alone pour
out our whole souls to Jesus. In like manner, when
David and Jonathan would embrace and kiss one
another, they not only retired into " the field "

without the city, but even waited until the lad that carried the arrows " was gone ;" and " *then* they kissed one another, and wept one with another, until David exceeded " (1 Sam. xx. 35, 41). Beautiful type of Christ, the true David, the *beloved* of his Bride! " There," she exclaims, " there will I give thee my loves !"

" Loves " is in the plural in the Hebrew, to shew the abundance and excellency of it. It is not simply *love*, but the highest degree, the excess, the over-flowings of love !

> Ver. 13. " *The mandrakes give a smell, and at our gates are all manner of pleasant fruits, new and old, which I have laid up for thee, O my beloved.*"

These words may either be taken as the con-tinued language of the Bride, or as the answer of Christ to her invitation to inspect her fruitfulness (ver. 11, 12).

If the Bride is still speaking, her words evidence a *very* advanced stage of Christian experience, that she should be able to make such a declaration in the spirit of humility—" At our gates are *all manner* of *pleasant fruits !*" But all idea of merit or self-exaltation is at once disclaimed in the following words —" which I have laid up *for thee*, O my beloved."

It is very certain that every development of the fruits of the Spirit in the Lord's people, and every act performed for his sake, is as treasure laid up in heaven for the Lord of the harvest. There is

no other allusion in Scripture to a believer's laying up *for Christ*. When we are exhorted to "lay
up," it is *for ourselves*—as in 1 Tim. vi. 18, 19; Matt.
vi. 20, and xix. 21—for we are receiving out of
Christ's fulness only *sufficient grace* for *daily use.*
(The laying up the tithe of increase every third
year, in Deut. xiv. 28, was a ministering to the need
of *others*, "the Levite, the stranger, and the father-
less," rather than a laying up for the Lord. And
it is the only other instance where the expression
occurs).

It seems, therefore, more probable that the words
are to be taken as Christ's reply to his Bride,
most graciously owning and accepting the sweet
fragrance he met with in his inspection of the vineyards—"The mandrakes give a smell."

But, as if he would give her no room for resting
in present attainments, and lest she should be satisfied with the sweetness of such holy experience in
this life, he immediately directs her to look yet
higher, adding, "And at our gates are all manner
of pleasant fruits, which I have laid up for thee, O
my beloved."

There is much yet "laid up." "O how great is
the goodness which thou hast *laid up* for them that
fear thee!" as well as that "which thou hast
wrought *before the sons of men!*" (Ps. xxxi. 19).
"There is *laid up* for me a crown of righteousness,"
&c. (2 Tim. iv. 8). Much is revealed to us now in
sweet foretastes, through the indwelling of the Spirit

of God (1 Cor. ii. 9, 10), but the full enjoyment of all is "*laid up*," "*reserved* in heaven" for us, to be known only in his presence where there is "*fulness* of joy!*"

Then, when we "enter in *through the gates* into the city" (Rev. xxii. 14), what wonders we shall know of that "*light* which no *man* can approach unto;" of that glory which "no *man* hath seen or can see;" and of that *kingdom* which "*flesh and blood* cannot inherit!" for there is "laid up" for us there, "*all manner* of pleasant fruits." "*Fulness* of joy —*pleasures* for evermore" (Ps. xvi. 11). "Thou shalt make *them* drink of the river *of thy pleasures!*" (Ps. xxxvi. 8.) Truly a glorious harvest is laid up for us in that heavenly garner, "where neither moth nor rust doth corrupt, and where thieves do not break through and steal."

There is yet one more thought of exceeding preciousness in the personal appropriation of all this —"for *thee*, O my beloved." Yes, for *me!* may every member of Christ's mystical body exclaim— "He loved *me*, and gave himself for *me*;" and if he is mine, *all things* are mine! it is all "laid up" for *me!*

> "Most wondrous joys he lets us know,
>   In fields and villages below;
>   Gives us a relish of his love—
>   But keeps his noblest feast above!

> "In Paradise within the gates,
>   A higher entertainment waits,
>   Fruits,* new and old, laid up in store,
>   Where we shall feed, but thirst no more."—WATTS.

* Lev. xxvi. 10.

CHAPTER VIII.

The Bride.

Ver. 1. "O that thou wert as my brother, that sucked the breasts of my mother!"

It seems so unlikely, towards the close of a book of Christian experience such as this, in the matured development of the Christian life, and after such strong and unhesitating language has been used of a relationship *still closer than a brother's*, that the Church should now exclaim with regard to *Christ*, "O that thou wert as my brother!" that it is far more reasonable to understand these words in reference to those who were "*without*" the vineyards which the Bride had been inspecting. From within that sacred enclosure, her eyes would rest on "the waste howling wilderness," in which were many who were yet strangers to God; and in the overflowings of a heart of love, which beat in unison with that of Jesus when *He* looked down from heaven with a pitying eye upon a world of rebels, she would be constrained to exclaim, "O that thou wert as my brother, that sucked the breasts of my mother!" She would earnestly desire for them that they were brought into the same family, as children of the same Father, and partakers of the same new birth with herself (the Holy Spirit being always understood, throughout the book, as the divine author of the new birth, under the term "mother"), and thus made with her to be *brethren* in the holy fellowship of the gospel.

This yearning desire after those who are "without," is only that *reflecting* of *the Lord's love* which is to be looked for in all who are vitally united to him. Do we not hear him say, "O Jerusalem, Jerusalem, how often would I have gathered thy children together!" &c. And again, "O that there were such an heart in them!" &c. (Matt. xxiii. 37; Deut. v. 29). It was in this spirit that so soon as Andrew had found Jesus, he sought his brother Simon, and "*brought him to Jesus*" (John i. 41, 42); and that Philip immediately afterwards invited Nathanael to "come and see" him also (ver. 45, 46). It was in the same spirit that St Paul declared he could wish himself accursed from Christ *for his brethren*, &c. (Rom. ix. 3), and that he was constantly in prayer "night and day" to bring his fellow-sinners to Jesus. The far-advanced believer having drank deeply into Christ's love, manifests proportionably his own love to others.

" *When I should find thee without, I would kiss thee ;
yea, I should not be despised.*"

Thus most beautifully following *in the track* of her
Beloved, who, when he saw the returning prodigal yet
" afar off," ran to meet him, and fell on his neck
and *kissed* him ! (Luke xv. 20.)   Jesus had dealt
thus *with her*, for she was once at a distance from
him, and she would, therefore, now " kiss " those
whom *she* found " without," " a great way off."
Nor would her labour be in vain in the Lord—
" Yea, I should not be despised."

Oh for more of this loving, earnest yearning of
spirit after those who are yet " without ! "   " Let us
consider one another to provoke unto love and to
good works."   It was thus the Bride delighted to
act.   " Not forsaking the *assembling of ourselves*
together, . . . but *exhorting* one another ; and so
much the more as ye see the day approaching"
(Heb. x. 24, 25).   She would fain have others to be
sharers of her joys.

Ver. 2. " *I would lead thee, and bring thee into
my mother's house.*"

I would not leave thee to perish, like the priest
and the Levite in the parable, passing by on the
other side (Luke x.), but I would seek to bring thee
to the ordinances and the dwelling-place of my
Beloved.   I would lead thee *into fellowship of spirit*
with myself.

Are we afraid to speak thus, and to say, " *I* would

lead thee," &c.?   Alas! too often the believer *is*
heard coldly affirming, " *I* cannot convert such an
one ; it is a work *I* have nothing to do with ; *I*
must leave that to God," &c. &c.   Truly, of himself
he is " not sufficient " for these things ; " but our
sufficiency is of God."   We do not go alone to the
work.   Wherever we go, we take Christ with us ;
" for we are one with Christ, and Christ with us."
If we speak, it is *not we* that speak, but the Spirit
of our Father which speaketh in us (Matt. x. 20).
If we win souls to Jesus, it is *because* the Father
draws them (John vi. 44).   If we seek, as Andrew
did, to lead an unconverted brother to Jesus, why
should we not, as he did, " *bring him* to Jesus ?"

Surely it is that we do not realise our oneness
with Christ in these things, or we should not have
" so little faith."   We, independently of him, could
do nothing ; but *he in us* must accomplish God's
purpose of love towards them who are " without."

   " *Who would instruct me.*"

Here lay the secret of her success : she was *taught
of the Spirit*, whose special office it is to " *teach* us
all things," and to " guide us into all truth " (John
xvi. 13, and xiv. 26).   " The Holy Ghost shall
teach you in the same hour *what ye ought to say* "
(Luke xii. 12).   It was thus with Stephen—" a man
full of the Holy Ghost ; " " they were *not able to
resist* . . . the Spirit *by which* he spake " (Acts vi.
5, 10).

Even the Lord Jesus was himself thus instructed " how to speak a word in season," &c. (Isa. l. 4, and xi. 2, 3). Learn then, believer, that if your body is the temple of the Holy Ghost which is in you, ye are to seek, " in the power of his might," to lead others to a like participation of the new birth. " I would lead thee," &c.

> " *I would cause thee to drink of spiced wine of the juice of my pomegranate.*"

We must not even be content to bring them into the fold, but we must let them *share our pasture.* We must impart willingly to them of the " bread enough *and to spare* " of our Father's house. For if the multitude of five thousand were still to be fed, there would still be " baskets of fragments " to take up. Thus (in Acts xviii. 25, 26) we read that Apollos being " *instructed* in the way of the Lord, . . . spake and taught diligently the things of the Lord." But Aquila and Priscilla were farther advanced ; and, in the spirit of the Bride, " they took him unto them, and expounded unto him the way of God more perfectly ; " thus making him to drink of their " spiced wine."

All this is a yet further reflection of the mind of Christ ; for does he not say, " I have drunk my wine with my milk : eat, O *friends*; drink, yea, drink abundantly, O *beloved*"? (chap. v. 1); " Come, drink of the wine which I have mingled " (Prov. ix. 5). Then is it most fitting in his Bride to say likewise,

" I would cause thee to drink of the spiced wine of
the juice of *my* pomegranate." Just what the literal
Israel were required to do literally, is required of
the spiritual seed spiritually. " Thou shalt furnish
him (thy brother) liberally . . . out of thy floor *and
out of thy wine press:* of that wherewith the Lord
thy God hath blessed thee, thou shalt give unto
him " (Deut. xv. 14).

Let us, then, invite others to share the precious
feast of good things, of which we have been made
partakers, saying, " Come with us, and we will do
thee good ; and what goodness the Lord shall do to
us, the same will we do to thee " (Numb. x. 29, 32).
For there need be no selfishness among Christians,
so long as there is " a *Fountain* of living waters" to
draw from. Nay, " he that watereth shall be
watered also himself." For "there is that scatter-
eth, *and yet increaseth* " (Prov. xi. 24, 25).

Ver. 3. " *His left hand should be under my head,
and his right hand should embrace me.*"

Beautiful picture of the soul peacefully resting in
the arms and on the bosom of Jesus ! It seems to
be the utterance of the Bride, *revelling,* as it were, in
the sweet consciousness of her nearness, her *closeness*
to Christ, rendered more sweet by the contrast of
those who were "afar off."

Thrice blessed repose ! " His left hand should be
under my head, and his right hand should embrace
me." The words seem to imply more than the

mere actual *present* experience of it, for there is
also the resting in the calm assurance that so it
" *should be.*" It was a privilege she claimed as her
own. She *had* experienced it before, and she *would
do so yet again.* She would feel his hand embracing
her, and keeping her within his own sacred enclosure.

It was in the mother's house now, as it had
been in the banqueting house before, that she had
been brought to this holy exercise of " leaning on
her beloved" (chap. ii. 4). But she was then
brought there, as it were, alone ; all her care and
concern was about herself : *now*, she is seen there
in company, as it were, with others whom she has
led thither to share her wine.

Then, too, in the warmth of " first love," the
manifestations of Christ were overwhelming to her
soul—" I am sick of love," she exclaimed ; " stay
me with flagons" (chap. ii. 5). But *now* there is
the holy calmness which characterises the more
matured believer, sweetly resting in the arms of
Jesus, not with less confidence and holy assurance
of soul, but without that ecstatic frame of mind.
It is always thus that, in the development of that
faith " which worketh by love," we learn to " look
also on the things of others," as we go ourselves
" from strength to strength."

CHRIST.

Ver. 4. " *I charge you, O daughters of Jerusalem,*

that ye stir not up, nor awake my love, until she *please.*"

The marginal reading of this verse may suggest to us that *now* this charge to the daughters of Jerusalem is *added to* by an appeal to themselves. "*Why* should ye stir up, or *why* awake my love till she please ?" As if they were now themselves awakened to some sense of the sweetness of religion, and ought, therefore, at once to understand the appeal.

The charge occurs (as in both the previous instances in chap. ii. 7, and iii. 5) whilst the Bride was in the enjoyment of peculiarly hallowed communion ; and it seems to teach us that such seasons are not broken in upon—save by our own consent ! —" until she please."

The verse immediately following suggests also that the believer cannot be always resting ; he is called aside to " *rest a while,*" from time to time, during his pilgrim journey ; but, after all, his must be *an onward course.*

Ver. 5. " *Who is this that cometh up from the wilderness.*"

Coming up — journeying — making progress. Such is the characteristic feature of the true believer. But from whence ? " From the *wilderness.*" Ah ! it is well to be taught to look back " to the rock whence we are hewn, and the hole of the pit whence we are digged." The Lord would not have us forget it at any stage of our experience. His *first* words and his *last* to his Bride were alike to call to her remembrance what she had been—a beggar raised from the dunghill to inherit the throne of glory, that the exceeding riches of his grace might be magnified in her. Thus, in chap. i. 9, he says, " I have compared thee, O my love, to a company of horses in Pharaoh's chariots," brought up *out of Egypt*; and now he asks, " Who is this that cometh up *from the wilderness?*" He knew her when it was her home !—" I did know thee *in the wilderness*, in the land of great drought;" "in the open field," &c. (Hos. xiii. 5 ; Ezek. xvi. 5). And full well did he keep in remembrance her "first love," manifested *there;* " I remember thee, the kindness of thy youth, the love of thine espousals, when thou wentest after me in the wilderness,'' &c. (Jer. ii. 2). And every step of her coming up from it he knows : " He knoweth thy walking through this great wilderness." " The *steps* of a good man are ordered by the Lord," &c. (Deut. ii. 7). And he knows the progress we make. He knows when we are drawing near the borders of the wilderness, when we are *nearly through* it ; when we are *coming up* from it ! Precious in his sight is the far-advanced believer—whose " wilderness" journey is almost finished—his toils, his sufferings, his conflicts, almost over. How he watches our *coming up from* the wilderness !

There is something like the language of holy

boasting in the expression, "*Who* is this that cometh up from the wilderness?" As if the Lord Jesus called attention to his beloved Bride whom he had tenderly protected under the shadow of his wings all through her perilous journey, and was now triumphantly bringing up from the wilderness, to convey her to his Father's house; for to him alone she owes her safety.

"*Leaning upon her beloved.*"

Yes! every other dependence has been renounced. She is bereft of every other stay. She advances in her onward course—"leaning on her beloved!" It is enough. She is abundantly supported: "underneath are the everlasting arms."

It may indeed appear to the worldling a strange sight; but the believer *in Jesus* can afford to lose all, if she may "win Christ." She can wander alone in the wilderness of this world, if needs be, for "forty years," and she will "lack nothing," for in Christ she has all, and abounds! (Deut. ii. 7). Like Moses, she *endures*, "as seeing him who is invisible;" like John, she breathes out every thought into the ear of her Beloved, "leaning on his bosom." And this is the secret of the sweet peace of the children of God: *they cling to the all-supporting stem of the "true vine."* Nothing can rend them asunder. The expression "leaning on" implies a sense of weakness. It is a word nowhere else used in Scripture, signifying a clinging to, or strengthening one's self upon another. So that our very feebleness is a divinely-appointed means for the display of " the power of his might." " My strength is made perfect *in weakness*." " Most gladly, therefore (may every believer say), will I rather glory in my infirmities, that the power of Christ may rest upon me" (2 Cor. xii. 9, 10). Let us, therefore, comfort one another with these words while *passing through the wilderness*. " Strangers and pilgrims !" having no continuing city to dwell in, compelled to pitch our tents up and down from time to time, while " wandering in the wilderness in a solitary way," yet " led forth by the right way," that we *may come* to a *city* of *habitation!* (Ps. cvii. 4, 7).

The Lord is oftentimes pleased to make the wilderness a specially chosen place of blessing to his beloved ones— " I will allure her, and bring her into the wilderness, and speak comfortably unto her" (Hos. ii. 14). For it is when most bereft of earthly things that we *most* enjoy the supporting and abiding presence of our " well beloved," and find him to be indeed our " *all* and *in all*."

There is also something peculiarly comforting in the Lord's *owning* of his Bride's appropriation of him ; " leaning on her beloved." It is like Hos. iii. 3—" Thou shalt not be for another man ; so will I also be *for thee*." He most jealously demands the *whole* heart, and most graciously owns it when it is given. He calls himself " her beloved."

"*I raised thee up under the apple-tree: there thy
mother brought thee forth: there she brought thee
forth that bare thee.*"

"I raised thee up." When thou wast *dead*, I
quickened thee (Eph. ii. 1–7). "I said unto thee
when thou wast in thy blood, Live" (Ezek. xvi. 3,
&c.) "I raised thee" from the bondage of Satan,
to "the glorious liberty of the children of God;"
"I raised thee" "from darkness to light, and from
the power of Satan unto God." It was *I* that raised
thee up. "I raised thee up under the apple-tree."
We have learnt from chapters ii., iii. the meaning
of "the apple-tree"—"As the apple-tree among the
(wild) trees of the wood, *so is my beloved* among the
sons." It is Jesus. For he is "the tree of life"—
"I am the resurrection and the life."

"There thy mother brought thee forth." Oh!
how wonderfully the believer is brought into fellowship with Jesus! Just as the Babe in Bethlehem
was "conceived of the Holy Ghost," so is the Christian spiritually *born of the Spirit*. We are made
new creatures in Christ Jesus by the agency of the
Holy Ghost. We are made the sons of God by
the Spirit of adoption. We are admitted into God's
family by the new birth of the Spirit—"There she
brought thee forth that bare thee." How powerfully these words recall the utterance of Jesus, in
the contemplation of what was to be the blessed
fruit of his sufferings and death! "Verily, verily,
I say unto you, Except a corn of wheat fall into the

ground and die, it abideth alone ; but if it die, it *bringeth forth much fruit*" (John xii. 24). " He shall see of *the travail* of his soul, and shall be satisfied " (Isa. liii. 11).

We are the children, the spiritual seed, thus brought forth — the fruit of the travail of his soul.

Raised up under the apple-tree.

" Contrast her state by nature and by grace : brought from under *the curse* under the first apple-tree in Eden, and placed under *the blessing* of the second apple-tree in the garden of covenant love."— MRS STEVENS.

The words may likewise apply to the *restoring* grace of Christ. Thus, in chapter ii. 3–5, the Bride was swooning and fainting through excess of spiritual joy ; but her Beloved raised her up, and stayed and supported her. So, again, under the scorching heat of the noonday sun, he filled her with resurrection power, while he was unto her " as a shadow from the heat ; " and, when parched with thirst, his fruit was sweet and reviving to her taste. " The leaves of the tree are for the *healing* of the nations." For it is not a withering gourd ; but a tree *of life, full of resurrection power !* vivifying and quickening. It was this power which wrought in the Bride when, in chapter iii. 1, 2, it caused her to cry out from her bed, " I will rise now," &c. And, again, in chapter v., when, after vain excusings of her inability to open to him, she was at length so constrained by his dealings of love, that she "*rose up to open to her beloved.*"

The same power wrought in the prodigal son in the far distant country, exciting in his heart the blessed determination, "*I will arise* and go to my father," &c. "*I raised thee up.*" Oh! how earnestly is the Christian, whose soul lies cleaving unto the dust, heard to exclaim with St Paul, " That I may know him *and the power of his resurrection* "—" That ye may know . . . what is the exceeding greatness of his power to us-ward who believe, according to the working of his mighty power, which he wrought in Christ when he *raised him* from the dead "—" and hath *raised us up together,*" &c. (Eph. i. 19, 20 ; and ii. 6, 7). " Blessed and holy is he that hath part in the first resurrection."

THE BRIDE.

Ver. 6. " *Set me as a seal upon thine heart, as a seal upon thine arm.*"

The figure of "a seal" suggests many precious thoughts.

First, Its primary reference is doubtless to the high priesthood of Jesus. In Exodus xxviii. we read, that on the breastplate of the high priest were engraven the names of the twelve tribes of the children of Israel, that Aaron might bear them "*on his heart* before the Lord continually" (ver. 15–30).

And again, that in the two stones of the ephod were to be engraven, "like the engravings of a signet," the names of the children of Israel, that Aaron might "bear their names before the Lord *upon his two shoulders* for a memorial" (ver. 6–12). And hence the prayer of the Bride—"Set me as a seal *upon thine heart,* as a seal *upon thine arm.*"

How inexpressibly delightful to the Church of Christ is the thought of "a great High Priest that is passed into the heavens, *Jesus* the Son of God," bearing now both on his heart and on his arm the names of all his spiritual Israel before the Lord! How sweet to be thus *sealed upon Jesus!*

Second, A seal is used for ratifying and confirming (see Neh. ix. 38; Rom. iv. 11). And the Bride thus betakes herself to the "strong consolation" provided in the promise and the oath of her Beloved, that the *covenant engagement* into which she has entered shall never be broken, and that she shall never depart from him (Jer. xxxii. 40; Hos. iii. 3).

Third, It is also a token of peculiar honour and affection. (Compare Jer. xxii. 24 with Haggai ii. 23.)

Fourth, A seal *leaves an impression,* and we are to be thus "conformed to the image of his Son," and *moulded* like wax or clay according to the device of "the potter."

Lastly, This sealing process is the peculiar office of the Holy Spirit—"whereby ye are sealed unto the day of redemption" (Eph. i. 13, 14 ; Eph. iv. 30 ; 2 Cor. i. 22).

The prayer of the Bride may include all these several thoughts. "Set me *as a seal*."

It is a prayer that breathes intense earnestness and fervent love, and has evidently an especial reference to the sealing or *making sure* (Matt. xxvii. 66) of that covenant engagement into which she had entered *with her Beloved*. "Set *me* as a seal upon *thine* heart ;" bind *me* to *thee* in the closest of all bonds, making *me* to adhere to *thee,* even as the wax to the parchment—"as a seal."

She would be sealed upon his "*heart*," where the *deepest* impression might be made upon his tender love and intense affection (Eph. iii. 18, 19) ; and likewise upon his "arm," that she might insure the exercise of all his omnipotence on her behalf (Ps. lxxvii. 15). "*Strong* is thine arm."

In both respects he has answered her prayer most wonderfully : "*I* will not forget thee—I have graven thee *on the palms of my hands*" (Isa. xlix. 15, 16). Again, "He shall gather the lambs with his arm, and carry them *in his bosom*"—"His *arm* shall rule for him" (Isa. xl. 10, 11). "The foundation of God standeth sure, having this seal, The Lord knoweth them that are his" (2 Tim. ii. 19).

"*For love is strong as death.*"

Jesus has testified to this truth in actual experience—"Greater *love* hath no man than this, that a man *lay down his life* for his friends." "And I lay down *my* life for the sheep." "Who *loved* me, and *gave himself* for me."

And since the Bride's love is but the reflection of his, hers *also* is "strong as death." "*For thy sake* we are killed all the day long," &c. (Rom. viii. 36; Acts xxi. 13). Therefore it is written of the noble army of martyrs, that "they loved not their lives unto the death" (Rev. xii. 11). "For the love *of Christ* constraineth *us*," &c. (2 Cor. v. 14, 15). "Love is strong as death." "Who shall separate us from the love of Christ? shall tribulation, or distress, or persecution, or famine, or nakedness, or peril, *or sword?* Nay, in all these things we are more than conquerors through him that loved us. For I am persuaded that *neither death*, nor life, . . . nor any other creature, shall be able to separate us from the love of God, which is in Christ Jesus our Lord" (Rom. viii. 35–39).

> " But drops of grief can ne'er repay
> The debt of love I owe ;
> Here, Lord, I give *myself* away—
> 'Tis all that I can do."

> " Love, so amazing, so divine,
> Demands my soul, my life, my all !"—WATTS.

" *Jealousy is cruel as the grave.*"

" The Lord thy God is a jealous God." He will bear no rival ; he will have the *whole* heart.

And forasmuch as " all his actions towards us

imprint their stamp in us" (MANTON), the believer is likewise, of necessity, filled with a holy jealousy towards Christ. He must have Christ *all to himself*; he cannot let other objects rival him in his heart. He is often heard to exclaim—

> " Do not I love thee, O my Lord?
> Behold my heart and see;
> And cast each cursed idol down,
> That dares to rival thee."—DODDRIDGE.

This "jealousy" is expressive of that intensity of appropriation which is the privilege of every individual believer; for such is our Beloved, that he is *all* to every one. And none loses by his entire appropriation by another! There is no diminution by participation.

Be jealous, then, believer, of the love of Jesus. Fear not to be "cruel as the grave" in thy demands upon it.

The grave is *never satisfied:* it says not, It is enough (Prov. xxx. 15, 16). Go and do thou likewise. *Crave* the love of Jesus.

> " Only the Fountain Head above
> Can satisfy *the thirst* of love."—NEWTON.

"Jealousy is cruel as the grave." "As the grave will not give up its dead, so neither will Jesus give up his own."

> " *The coals thereof are coals of fire, which hath a most vehement flame.*" (Heb., " *The coals thereof are the flames of the fire of the Lord.*")

"Coals of fire"—elsewhere called " *live coals*"

(see Isa. vi. 6). "Then flew one of the seraphims unto me, having *a live coal* in his hand, . . . taken from *off the altar*," kindled by the Lord himself. The fire is his, and the coals are his. So is it most emphatically with Christian love.

It is in its essence kindled in heaven—it is "*the love of the Spirit*" (Rom. xv. 30)—Christ's own love pervading (through the indwelling of his Spirit) all the members incorporate in his mystical body.

"The flames of the fire of the Lord." Alas! wherefore are they so often like to "smoking flax" rather than to fiery flames, burning so brightly that all might *see* their light, and *feel* their heat? Why do we reflect so little of the flaming love of Jesus? Is it not because we have so little "delight in drawing near God, and *warming* our *souls at the fire of his love?*"—CHARNOCK.

No other coals than those *kindled by the Lord* can avail to keep alive this holy love within our hearts. "The coals thereof are coals of fire, which are *the flames* of *the fire* of *the Lord.*" The original Hebrew word in this place is compounded of three words—"fire, flame, and Jah." And it is remarkable that it is the only time the name of God occurs throughout the book.

Patrick thinks there is an allusion to (Lev. vi. 12, 13) the fire which was ever burning on the altar. If it be so, we are at once reminded how entirely that flame *consumed* the sacrifice. The burnt-offering was frequently expressed by the Hebrew word *olah*, *i. e.*, "*an ascension*," from the whole sacrifice being consumed, and going up in a flame to the Lord. And how truly Jesus *was* thus consumed by this "vehement flame" of love! O to understand more of its height, and depth, and length, and breadth! "Love is strong as death." It "passeth knowledge" (Eph. iii. 17–19).

> Ver. 7 "*Many waters cannot quench love, neither can the floods drown it.*"

If love is a flame of the fire of the Lord, it is a fire no waters can quench. Though all his "waves and billows" go over our heads—though floods of persecution assail us—"though the waters roar and be troubled"—yea, though we *pass* "*through the waters*," yet, sheltered in Christ, the true Ark, we shall but rise higher and higher *upon* the waters; for nothing, *nothing* "shall separate us from *the love* of God which is in Christ Jesus our Lord." It shall rather be as in the days of Elijah, that although the water be poured upon the sacrifice over and over again, till it fill even the trench round about the altar, still "the fire of the Lord" shall *lick up the water* in the trench! (1 Kings xviii. 33–38); for "many waters cannot quench love."

If the flames of hell are spoken of as an "unquenchable fire," how much *more* so are the flames *of love* kindled *in heaven!* "Charity *never* faileth" (1 Cor. xiii.)

And if the love of Jesus carried him through such deep, *deep waters* for our sakes, how should the remembrance of that love carry us through all the *smaller streams* which lie in our way, for the love we have to him!

> "Come, Holy Spirit, Heavenly Dove,
>   With all thy quickening powers;
> Come, shed abroad a Saviour's love,
>   And that shall kindle ours."

" If a man would give all the substance of his house for love, it would utterly be contemned."

What a powerful argument this was in the mouth of the Bride of Christ! She would be sealed upon his heart, and upon his arm, that nothing might separate them. She would be bound to him in indissoluble bonds—and the tie that bound them must be *love*.

For even in earthly connexions, she argues, nothing a man could give would be accepted, if he withheld his love. " If a man would give all the substance of his house for love, it would utterly be contemned." Shall they, then, who have yielded their affections to the Lord, be satisfied with less? God forbid! Even heaven itself, *the " Father's house*," would be utterly contemned, with all its ten thousand times ten thousand enjoyments over and above all earthly good, *were the love of Jesus wanting there!*

Oh! it is the being sealed on *the heart* of Jesus that believers crave after—*on his heart of love!*

O

" Do not I love thee from my soul ?
    Then let me nothing love !
Dead be my heart to every joy,
    When *Jesus* cannot move.

" Would not my heart shed all its blood
    In honour of thy name ?
And challenge the cold hand of *death*
    To damp the *immortal flame ?*"—DODDRIDGE.

" Then, Lord, *thy* love to me impart,
    And seal my name upon *thy* heart ;
Seal me upon thine arm, and wear
    That pledge of love for ever there."—WATTS.

This fervour of love is no mere passion ; it is no mere outbreak of enthusiasm ; it is a deep and lively *reality.* It is a spark from the flame of the strong and active love of Jesus. It manifests itself in its actings towards others.

Ver. 8. " *We have a little sister, and she hath no breasts : what shall we do for our sister in the day when she shall be spoken for ?*"

There seems to be the same yearning after family relationship here as in verse 1—" O that thou wert *as my brother !*" " We have a little *sister*, and she hath no breasts."

The Bride is no longer wholly absorbed with her own individual necessities ; her one inquiry is no longer, " What must *I* do to be saved ?" nor her one desire, " Lord, that *I* might receive *my* sight" —" God be merciful to *me*, a sinner"—" Lord, remember *me*," &c. — " Sir, give *me* this living water," &c. She is able now to "look also on the things of others." For when we have tasted for

ourselves of that "living water," we shall be ready
to leave our own water-pot, like the Samaritan
woman, and go into the city, and invite our friends,
saying, "Come, see a man," &c. (John iv. 28, 29).
When our eyes have been opened, we shall begin
to inquire, with St Paul, "Lord, what wilt thou
have me to do?" For we are not to follow the
Lord selfishly—we must go home to our friends,
and tell them what great things he hath done for
us. We must be willing to "spend, and be
spent," for the good of others ; yea, and even rejoice to be "poured forth" for the service of their
faith ! (Phil. ii. 17, marg. ; Mark v. 19; 2 Cor. xii.
15).

It was thus with the Bride. She felt that there
were yet many "daughters of Jerusalem" who were
not espoused to Christ. They did not stand to him
in the same relation that she did. "We have a
little sister," but she is *not yet* "*married* to another,
even to him who is raised from the dead, that she
should bring forth fruit unto God" (Rom. vii. 4 ;
contrast chapter vii. 7, 8). "What shall we *do* for
our sister?" is therefore her anxious inquiry. Oh !
to be often breathing out this language in the ear
of Jesus ! "*What* wilt thou have me to do?"
"Cause me to know the way wherein I should
walk."—"Make thy way *plain* before my face."
We cannot do God's work without God's direction
in doing it.

Nor is direction sought in vain. "I will shew

thee what thou shalt do," is his gracious assurance (Acts ix. 6 ; 1 Sam. xvi. 3 ; Ps. xxxii. 8).

The expression, " *in the day* when she shall be spoken for," implies that a work *was to be done* in the Lord's time. It also involves the idea of working " *while it is day*"—while we have " opportunity," &c. (Gal. vi. 10). For if " the day" be lost, " the night cometh when no man can work" (John ix. 4). May the Lord's servants be always " *ready to do* " whatsoever he appoints (2 Sam. xv. 15), " in the day" when he has designed to shew favour.

> Ver. 9. " *If she be a wall, we will build upon her a palace of silver: and if she be a door, we will inclose her with boards of cedar.*"

These two expressions may denote two different states or conditions—" *a wall* " being a work begun and in progress, whilst " *a door* " implies only a readiness for that work. In 1 Cor. xvi. 9, we read of " a great door and effectual" being opened ; and in Phil. i. 6, that " he who *hath begun* a good work in you will perform it," &c.

Thus the Bride desired to build wisely, as she had opportunity. If " a door " presented itself, a way of access, she would be zealous, like St Paul, of " entering in " (2 Cor. ii. 12 ; 1 Thess. i. 9). " If she be a door, we will inclose her with boards of cedar "—" I would lead thee and *bring thee into* my mother's house " (ver. 2), inclosing thee within the gospel net, and bringing thee into Christian fellowship.

But, " if she be a wall, we will build upon her a palace of silver." When the foundation *is laid*, the building may be reared up : " building up yourselves on your most holy faith "—" rooted and built up in him " (Jude 20 ; Col. ii. 7). This building up is most important work ; " ye are built up a spiritual house," " for an habitation of God through the Spirit " (1 Pet. ii. 5 ; Eph. ii. 19, 22).

Babes in Christ must be " fed with milk, and not with meat," and must be cherished " even as a nurse cherisheth her children " (1 Cor. iii. 1, 2 ; 1 Thess. ii. 7). But where the work has made any progress, we are exhorted to give all diligence to *add* grace to grace (2 Pet. i. 4–11).

This the Bride desired to do. She manifested the blessed fruits of the Spirit's teaching ("who would instruct me," ver. 2), for her love abounded yet more and more, " in *knowledge* and in *all judgment*" (Phil. i. 9).

Ver. 10. " *I am a wall, and my breasts like towers.*"

She now contrasts her state with theirs : " I am a wall, and *my* breasts like towers." Already the building has attained a considerable height, it has reached unto the " towers." It is near upon completion. The foundation, which is Christ, has been laid, and the lively stones are being " daily *added* to the Church."

But although the " wall " has still to be built, as in Nehemiah's days, in the midst of enemies, so that the builders need to be girt with the sword of the Spirit, yet the good work which is begun shall be performed unto the day of Christ; and very soon " he shall bring forth the head-stone thereof with shoutings, crying, Grace, grace unto it!" (Zech. iv. 7).

" I am a wall." Thrice blessed acknowledgment! There is no hesitating, no doubting about it. It is not " *if* I be a wall," for the Bride uses no " *if*" in regard to her own condition. But rather, in full assurance of faith, she gratefully owns, to the glory of the Divine Architect, " I *am* a wall, and my breasts like towers." " Rooted and built up—*in him.*"

" *Then was I in his eyes as one that found favour.*"

We have a beautiful illustration of these words in Ezek. 16. The Lord found his Bride originally " cast out in the open field." But since he had passed by her, and looked upon her, and had entered into covenant with her, she had " increased and waxen great, and come to excellent ornaments : her *breasts* were *fashioned,* and her time was the time of love." She had " prospered exceedingly," and was become " exceeding beautiful."

" *Then* " was she in his eyes " as one that found

favour." " Hail! thou that art *highly favoured*," &c. (Luke i. 28).

It was beautifully figured also in Esther's history. Now it came to pass, on the third day, when Esther had put on her royal apparel, and the king saw her standing in the court, " that she *obtained favour* in his sight," &c. (Esther v. 1, 2).

How wonderful that sinners should find "favour" in the eyes of the King of kings! " They got not the land in possession by their own sword, neither did their own arm save them," is the divine interpretation of this holy mystery; " but thy right hand, and thine arm, and the light of thy countenance, *because thou hadst a favour unto them*" (Ps. xliv. 3). It is all God's free grace and " favour." He builds us up, and then takes delight in the building. He makes us to prosper, and then " hath pleasure " *in* our prosperity (Gen. xxxix. 3; Ps. xxxv. 27). He makes us fruitful, and then we find favour in his eyes because we are so! " Then was I in his eyes as one that found favour."

Thrice blessed is the soul that has learnt to rest satisfied with God's approval!—" *accepted* in the beloved." It is enough—" It is God that justifieth —who is he that condemneth?" If we have " found favour " in *his* eyes, what more can we need? This was the plea of Jesus—" Preserve my soul, for I am one *whom thou favourest*" (Ps. lxxxvi. 2, marg.) And what can we desire more for ourselves than to be remembered with the favour which God beareth unto his people ? (Ps. cvi. 4, 5).

Oh for a blessed *consciousness* of having thus found favour ! It seems to be the special privilege of the far-advanced believer, who can confidently affirm, " I am a wall, and my breasts like towers." " THEN," and perhaps not till then—not until we have decided evidences that we are in very deed the espoused ones of Jesus, can we assure ourselves that we have found favour in his eyes. " Beloved, if our heart condemn us not, then have we confidence toward God " (1 John iii. 20, 21).

Ver. 11. " *Solomon had a vineyard at Baal-hamon : he let out the vineyard unto keepers.*"

The truths connected with this " vineyard " are most deeply precious ; but, in sovereign wisdom, they are not unfolded till the believer has learnt, by dear-bought experience, to look entirely away from self, and to rest *solely* on the Lord Jesus and his finished work for acceptance and salvation. Christians are not set to work for God in order to merit God's favour. God forbid ! But when they have found favour in his eyes, and when they have carefully seen to the well-being of their *own* vineyard (see chapter vii. 12), *then* he sets them to be the keepers of his vineyard. This is very powerfully taught us in the conclusion of this book. We have seen the onward progress of Christian experience marked out in its various stages, the gradual development of spring, summer, and autumnal fruits ; and now, in the close of that experience, the ripened and matured believer is taught *to labour* in his Lord's vineyard ; and is reminded that his labour shall not be in vain in the Lord !

"Solomon had a vineyard at Baal-hamon." Our Solomon is Jesus, the King of kings, the true and only Potentate, &c. (1 Tim. vi. 14–16); and his vineyard is the Church. It is "a vineyard in a very fruitful hill" (Is. v. 1, &c.) ; for such is the literal meaning of the figurative expression, "a vineyard at Baal-hamon." "Baal" signifies one that possesses or rules ; "hamon" signifies multitude or riches. Jesus then is the ruler and owner of a very fruitful vineyard ! "Very fruitful !"—whether the *numbers* of "*trees* of righteousness" of his own right hand planting be referred to, or "the *fruits* of righteous- ness" which they bring forth abundantly by Jesus Christ to the glory and praise of God. The multi- tude of fruit trees, and the riches of his flock, have already been described. "Thy plants are an orchard of pomegranates, with pleasant fruits—with all trees of frankincense, and with all the chief spices," &c. (chap. iv. 13, 14). And again, "Thy teeth are like a flock of sheep, . . . whereof every one bear twins, and none is barren among them" (chap. iv. 2). "Herein is my Father glorified, that ye bear *much fruit*" (John xv. 8).

Such, then, is *our* Solomon's vineyard at Baal- hamon ! How blessed to be planted in it !—fenced about, interceded for, pruned, and purged.

But we are not planted in the Lord's garden to
be cumberers of the ground. Like Adam and Eve
in Eden, we are "to till the ground—to dress it
and to keep it" (Gen. ii. 5, 15). " He let out the
vineyard *unto keepers.*"   In one sense Jesus only is
" the dresser of the vineyard." He says of it, "*I
the Lord do keep it; I* will water it every moment :
lest any hurt it, *I* will *keep it* night and day" (Isa.
xxvii. 1–3). And well is it for us that it is safely
lodged in *his* keeping who neither slumbers nor
sleeps, but keeps it night and day. For had it been
given out of his hands into ours, we had lost it as
soon as Adam and Eve lost Paradise !

But Jesus and his Bride are one ; and in this
sense *we* are constituted " keepers." He commits
his goods into our hands as servants and stewards,
giving " to every man his work " (Mark xiii. 34),
and adding the solemn injunction, "*occupy* till I
come" (Luke xix. 13).

Dress the vineyard and keep it, is his charge to
each individual believer, as well as to the shepherds
and pastors of his flock. " Feed thy kids beside
the shepherds' tents" (chap. i. 8), is his universal
admonition. " Feed my lambs "—" Go ye into all
the world, and preach the gospel to every creature "
—" *Keep yourselves* in the love of God " (Jude 21).

> " *Every one for the fruit thereof was to bring a
> thousand pieces of silver.*"

Once the Lord of the vineyard let it out unto

husbandmen who would *not* yield him the fruit thereof; and what then did he do? He "let out his vineyard unto *other* husbandmen which should *render him* the *fruits in their seasons*" (Matt. xxi. 33, &c.) Jesus is looking for these fruits in each one of us. He looks for the tender grape and the green figs of spring; for the spices and pleasant fruits of summer; and for *the nuts* in autumn (see chaps. ii., iv., vi.) Are we then bringing forth these "fruits in their seasons" to render unto Jesus? "What shall *we* render unto the Lord?" What does he expect?

"Every one for the fruit thereof was to bring a thousand pieces of silver." The vineyard is planted on a very fruitful hill, and the Lord expects it to yield him a rich and very abundant produce. To whom he has given five talents, from him he expects "other five;" and to whom he has given two, from him he expects "two talents more." For "the manifestation of the Spirit is given to every man *to profit withal*" (1 Cor. xii. 7). Whatsoever God intrusts us with, be it wealth, or talents, or knowledge, or influence, it is not ours to use as we please—it must be *traded with*; it is given us "to *profit* withal."

Not to use it thus is robbery of God; for we then cannot have sufficient fruit to yield him the required produce. Oh that we more diligently sought to render unto him "the glory *due* unto his name!"

It is altogether a false and deceptive humility to
say, "But *my* poor works can bring no glory to
God," &c. &c.

Of course *our own* works, if they are offered like
Cain's sacrifice of the fruit of the soil, of our own
hearts, can never yield produce acceptable to Jesus.
But, if we are "*trees* of righteousness," planted by
God in his own vineyard, we *must* be more or less
" filled with *the fruits* of righteousness, which are by
Jesus Christ, unto the glory and praise of God."
For every good tree bringeth forth good fruit. And
of these fruits (with which, indeed, it becomes us to
" covet earnestly " to be well "*filled*") the whole
produce must be rendered to the Lord. " Every
one for the fruit thereof was to bring a thousand
pieces of silver." " Render unto God the things
which are God's." Let us trade with our talents
diligently — increase them " a hundred-fold," *and
then go and cast the price at Jesus' feet.* Keep back
none of the price of the land.

Ver. 12. " *My vineyard, which is mine, is before
me.*"

The Bride is not now a keeper of the vineyards
of others, to the neglect of her own (contrast chap.
i. 6). She is seen here diligently overlooking the
vineyard given *her* to keep. " My vineyard, which
is mine, is before me." The words indicate a strong
feeling of *personal* responsibility—a full consciousness of her own specific interest in her Lord's vine-

yard ; nor was she ignorant of his gracious purpose of rewarding " those that keep the fruit."

> " *Thou, O Solomon, must have a thousand, and those that keep the fruit thereof two hundred.*"

" A thousand pieces of silver" is God's demand, as the price of the produce of the vineyard. That, therefore, the Bride, as a faithful steward, will render unto him. And what Christian would not rejoice to cast his crown at the feet *of Jesus,* and to yield him all the glory of all the precious fruits of the Spirit wrought out in his experience ? " Whatsoever ye do, do it heartily as to the Lord, and not unto men, knowing that of the Lord ye shall receive *the reward* of *the inheritance ;* for ye serve the Lord Christ " (Col. iii. 23, 24).

" Receive the reward ?" Yes ! " those that keep the fruit " must have " two hundred." For " if any man's work abide which he hath built thereupon " (*i. e.* upon the foundation, Christ Jesus), " he shall receive a reward " (1 Cor. iii. 14). This is a very precious truth, and it is *not* dangerous, as some imagine, if it be truly understood. There is no danger of ascribing ought of this to human merit, if it be once for all distinctly seen and borne in mind, that " *the fruit*" is itself " *the fruit of the Spirit*" (Gal. v. 22), springing solely out of the vital union of the fruit-bearing branches *to the vine* (John xv.) God gives us " the *seed* " (2 Cor. ix. 10). He gives us " *the increase*" (1 Cor. iii. 6). " The *fruits* of righteousness are *by Jesus Christ*" (Phil. i. 11); and when he rewards, he rewards *his own work.* "Where is boasting then?" Oh! is it not for ever excluded? Do we not see that God gets himself glory by what he does in us? And is it the less his doing because he works *in us?* God forbid! The reward is not of debt, *but of grace.* For we are not only servants, but *also sons:* "and if sons, *then heirs.*" And yet we "shall receive the *reward* of the inheritance." "Those that keep the fruit" shall have "two hundred"—"for to him that hath *shall more* be *given*, and he shall have abundance."

When God has taught us the danger of looking to anything in ourselves as deserving of recompence, then he shews us that even a cup of cold water given *for his sake* shall in no wise lose its reward (Matt. x. 42); that, "whatsoever a man soweth, *that* shall he also reap" (Gal. vi. 7); and that, being rich in good works, we are laying up for ourselves a good foundation against the time to come (1 Tim. vi. 18, 19).

The sum specified is also replete with interest. "Two hundred"—that is precisely the fifth part of "a thousand;" in other words, it is two-tenths, or *a double tithe.* The sum God always demanded of Israel was "a tithe" of all that they had; but when he gives he does not give grudgingly—his reward is *a double tithe!*

"Thou, O Solomon, must have a thousand; and those that keep the fruit thereof two hundred."

We are reminded here of another scene in Old
Testament history. In Gen. xliii. 34, we read that
" Benjamin's mess was *five times so much* as any of
theirs." And the Lord Jesus here gets " five times
as much " as any of his brethren. We share his
joy, though in all things he has " the pre-eminence."
We yield *him all*—and he showers back upon us the
rich reward of a double tithe ! " For God is not
unrighteous to forget your work and labour of love,
which ye have shewed toward his name, in that ye
have ministered to the saints, and do minister "
(Heb. vi. 10).

Ver. 13. " *Thou that dwellest in the gardens, the
companions hearken to thy voice: cause me to
hear it.*"

" The Lord's throne is in heaven," yet he dwelleth
in " the garden " of his Church, among the trees
which his own hand hath planted. Time was when
the Bride imagined that her Beloved had forsaken
his garden and had " *turned aside*," but now she can
say, " Thou that *dwellest* in the gardens ! " This
acknowledgment bespeaks in her a calm and settled
assurance of mind, which she did not always possess.
It proves her to have *increased* in the knowledge of
her Lord and Saviour Jesus Christ.

Our eyes may at times be " holden," as Mary's
were at the sepulchre, when " she knew not that it
was Jesus," supposing him to have been the gardener ; but it is the privilege of the believer, in the

exercise of faith, to *know* that *Jesus is still there,* whether we see him or not. And we need but to hear his well-known "*voice*" saying, "Mary," to regain all our confidence, and have every suspicious fear put to flight.

The Bride therefore prays, "Thou that dwellest in the gardens, the companions hearken *to thy voice:* cause *me* to hear it."

"The word *companions* being in the masculine gender in the original, proves them to be the companions of the Bridegroom. His companions are '*the angels,* that excel in strength, and do his commandments,' having also this peculiar characteristic, '*hearkening unto the voice of his word*' (Ps. ciii. 20)." —DURHAM.

They always hear the voice of Jesus, and are ever ready to obey the first whisper of his word. Unlike the Bride, they never slumber; they never need to be aroused from off their beds; they never compel their Lord to stand at the door and *knock,* "saying, Open to me" (chaps. iii. and v.); they need no urging on to holy service; it is their delight to "do his commandments." They require no exhortation to listen when he speaks, for it is their incessant occupation to be "hearkening to the voice of his word!" And the Bride would fain "hear it," even as they. "Cause *me* to hear it"—give me to hear the "still small voice" speaking in thy gospel, in thy Word, in thy providences, in thy sanctuary and ordinances, *and in my daily walk.* "Speak comfortably" unto

me (Isa. xl. 2 ; Hos. ii. 14). Cause me to hear thy
voice—*even thine*, and *not* " the voice of a stranger ; "
the *shepherd's* voice (John x. 3–5, 27)—the *master's*
voice (1 Sam. iii. 9)—the *counsellor's* voice (Isa. xxx.
21)—the *reprover's* voice (Hab. ii. 1)—the *Father's*
voice (Heb. xii. 5)—and, above all, " *the voice of my
beloved.*" Cause me to hear it—" not for a time, but
for ever," even as do the angels. May converse
with Jesus be *my* happy employment, " hearkening
to the voice of his word." " Cause me," *thy Bride*,
" to hear it." This emphatic " me " again reminds
us of *the oneness* of the whole body of believers ;
" My dove, my undefiled is one." All the plants in
Christ's garden hear the voice of Jesus. Oh for
more of the *constant whisperings of the Spirit of Jesus*
in our hearts, quickening the drowsy, strengthening
the feeble, comforting the disconsolate. Why do we
not more earnestly reiterate the cry, " Thou that
dwellest in the gardens, the companions hearken to
thy voice : cause *me* to hear it "?

" The sheep hear his voice."

" Speak, Lord, for thy servant *heareth.*"

But the Bride of Jesus cannot stop here : sweet
indeed it is, while she is absent from her Beloved,
to listen to the breathings of his Spirit " in the
gardens," and to have Christ *dwelling* in her heart
by faith. But she urges yet one plea more.

Ver. 14. " *Make haste, my beloved, and be thou like
to a roe or to a young hart upon the mountains
of spices.*"   P

"Come, Lord Jesus." 'Tis true we have "the earnest of the Spirit in our hearts;" but we want, oh, we earnestly long for, "the appearing" of our Beloved upon the mountains of spices. "Make haste, my beloved, be thou like to a roe or to a young hart." Come swiftly, oh, "make haste!"

Such are the fervent breathings of the soul after Jesus!—such the intense affection of his Bride! How her language betrays the warmth of love! What holy vehemence she displays! One might wonder that sinners should dare to use such language towards their God; but "perfect love casteth out fear." And the Bride is now so filled with "the *full assurance* of faith," "*confidence* toward God," and *a love* which no waters can quench, that she bursts forth into this glowing language, "Make haste, my beloved!" even as one of old did dare to reiterate the same cry in one short Psalm *four* times over!—
"Make haste unto me, O God"—"O Lord, make no tarrying"—"Make haste, O God, to deliver me"—
"Make haste to help me, O Lord!" (Ps. lxx.)

Nor do the children of God desire less to see the Beloved of their souls, "as they see *the day* approaching." Hear the language of one: "When shall I be satisfied with thy face? When shall I be drunk with thy pleasures? Come, Lord Jesus, and tarry not. The Spirit says, *Come*—the Bride says, *Come:* even so, Lord Jesus, come quickly, and tarry not."
—J. WELSH.

And another writes: "Oh, how long is it to the

dawning of the marriage-day ? Oh, sweet Jesus, *take wide steps!* Oh, my Lord, *come over the mountains at one stride!* Oh, my blessed, flee as a roe or young hart upon the mountains of separation!" "Oh, time, run, run, and hasten the marriage-day, for love is tormented with delays!" And again, "I laugh, I smile, I leap for joy, to see Christ coming to save you so quickly. Oh, such wide steps as Christ taketh! Three or four hills are but a step to him. He skippeth over mountains."—S. RUTHERFORD.

Yea, and many can add, "My soul longeth, yea, *even fainteth,*" for the sight of Jesus !

> "The minutes seem to move too slow :
> May Jesus quickly come!"—WATTS.

"Be thou like to a roe or to a young hart upon the mountains of spices." It is not here, as in earlier experience, "the *mountains of Bether,*" or division (chap. ii. 17, margin)—it is not that clouds have come between us and Jesus, and we want to see the light of his countenance again by faith—no : the soul is here in the full possession of that bright and happy experience; but far above and beyond all that, yea, even while "our conversation *is* in heaven," we long for more still—"*we look for the* Saviour, the Lord Jesus Christ," &c. (Phil. iii. 20, 21). We look for his coming again to receive us unto himself; and this is something beyond our going to be with him. "Beloved, *now are we* the sons of God," says the apostle, BUT "it doth not yet appear *what we shall be :* but we know that, *when he shall appear*, we shall be like him; for we shall see him as he is" (1 John iii. 2). That is the consummation we are looking for.

> " One *view* of J sus as he is
> Will strike all sin for ever dead."—COWPER.

" We would *see* Jesus," is the ceaseless cry of his Bride. We are already upon "the mountains of spices"—we are already enjoying much of the heights and depths of the love of Jesus—already we are risen in him far above all the fading vanities of earth, which gradually appear smaller and fainter, and sink into real insignificance *as we ascend the mountain heights*, and leave them far behind in the plains below—already we seem to breathe something of the air of heaven, with its rich perfumes and spices—we are "sick of love"—we long to fly away, to see Jesus coming *in the clouds*, and to be "caught up to meet him in the air!" We long to be in glory,

> " Where saints in full fruition prove
> His rich *variety of love!* "—WATTS.

Oh! Christians, awake! " Arise ye, and depart, for this is not your rest." Get ye up into the "mountains of spices;" soar far above the grovelling things of sense; "*look up*, and lift up your heads." Get ye to the mountain-top, above all the *mists* of earth, that ye may clearly discern the first rays of light which shall mark the rising beams of the Sun of Righteousness. Stand upon your watch-tower — " Be ye ready" — " Watching unto prayer" — " Without spot" — "Unblameable." "Be found of him in peace" — " Let your loins be girded about, and your lights burning, and ye yourselves like unto men that *wait* for their lord" — " Looking for and hasting unto the coming of the day of God" — " Looking for that blessed hope, and the glorious appearing of the Great God, and our Saviour Jesus Christ" — and *abiding in him*, that when he shall appear ye may have confidence, and not be ashamed before him at his coming.

Yes! it is for that soul only which counts all things else *but loss* for *Christ* to be able in sincerity to echo the cry of the Bride, " Make haste, my beloved !" — " Why is his chariot so long in coming ? and why tarry the wheels of his chariot ?" Oh, listen to the gracious interpretation he has given of his delay — " The Lord is not slack concerning his promise, . . . *but is longsuffering to us-ward, not willing that any should perish, but that all should come to repentance*" (2 Pet. iii. 9).

> " Sinners still thy garments touching,
> *Stay thee* in thy coming here."

Enter, then, into fellowship of spirit with Jesus : and, by prayer and supplication, by life and conversation, seek to bring in those that are " without," and beseech him " shortly to accomplish the number of his elect." *So* shall he hasten his kingdom, and " so shall we ever be with the Lord." " Like a roe or a young hart," Jesus is drawing nigh. Hear his own voice, speaking to thee " in the gardens," and saying, " Surely I come quickly."

And may the same Spirit which breathes through him in those precious words (which make known *the mind of Christ* towards us) breathe through us also, as the vitally-united members of his body, causing us to cry out in oneness of spirit with him—" Amen ! Even so. come Lord Jesus !"

THE END.

BALLANTYNE, PRINTER, EDINBURGH.

Trieste

Trieste Publishing has a massive catalogue of classic book titles. Our aim is to provide readers with the highest quality reproductions of fiction and non-fiction literature that has stood the test of time. The many thousands of books in our collection have been sourced from libraries and private collections around the world.

The titles that Trieste Publishing has chosen to be part of the collection have been scanned to simulate the original. Our readers see the books the same way that their first readers did decades or a hundred or more years ago. Books from that period are often spoiled by imperfections that did not exist in the original. Imperfections could be in the form of blurred text, photographs, or missing pages. It is highly unlikely that this would occur with one of our books. Our extensive quality control ensures that the readers of Trieste Publishing's books will be delighted with their purchase. Our staff has thoroughly reviewed every page of all the books in the collection, repairing, or if necessary, rejecting titles that are not of the highest quality. This process ensures that the reader of one of Trieste Publishing's titles receives a volume that faithfully reproduces the original, and to the maximum degree possible, gives them the experience of owning the original work.

We pride ourselves on not only creating a pathway to an extensive reservoir of books of the finest quality, but also providing value to every one of our readers. Generally, Trieste books are purchased singly - on demand, however they may also be purchased in bulk. Readers interested in bulk purchases are invited to contact us directly to enquire about our tailored bulk rates. Email: customerservice@triestepublishing.com

You May Also Like

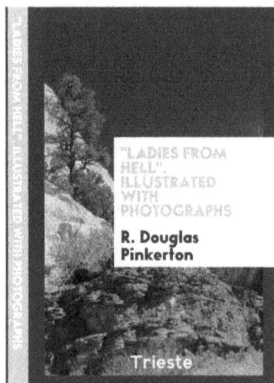

"Ladies from Hell".
Illustrated
with Photographs

R. Douglas Pinkerton

ISBN: 9781760573447
Paperback: 290 pages
Dimensions: 6.0 x 0.61 x 9.0 inches
Language: eng

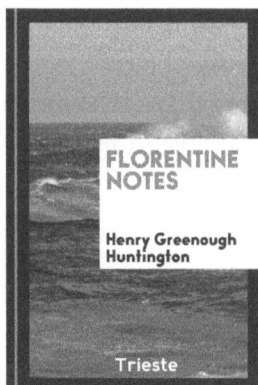

Florentine
Notes

Henry Greenough
Huntington

ISBN: 9781760579791
Paperback: 118 pages
Dimensions: 6.14 x 0.25 x 9.21 inches
Language: eng

You May Also Like

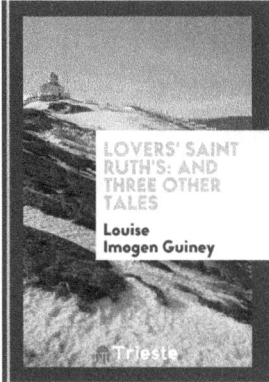

Lovers' Saint Ruth's: And Three Other Tales

Louise Imogen Guiney

ISBN: 9781760579814
Paperback: 144 pages
Dimensions: 5.83 x 0.31 x 8.27 inches
Language: eng

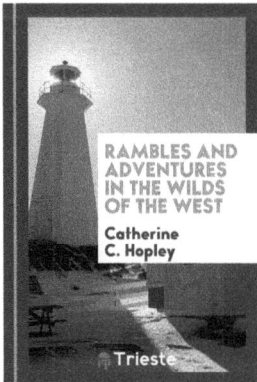

Rambles and Adventures in the Wilds of the West

Catherine C. Hopley

ISBN: 9781760579807
Paperback: 140 pages
Dimensions: 6.14 x 0.30 x 9.21 inches
Language: eng

www.triestepublishing.com

You May Also Like

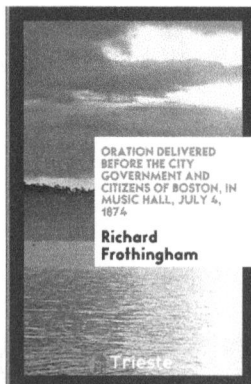

Oration delivered before the city government and citizens of Boston, in Music hall, July 4, 1874

Unknown

ISBN: 9780649010837
Paperback: 62 pages
Dimensions: 6.14 x 0.13 x 9.21 inches
Language: eng

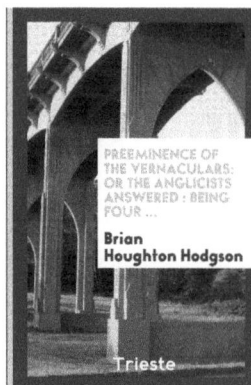

Preeminence of the Vernaculars: Or The Anglicists Answered : Being Four ...

Unknown

ISBN: 9780649019762
Paperback: 96 pages
Dimensions: 6.14 x 0.20 x 9.21 inches
Language: eng

You May Also Like

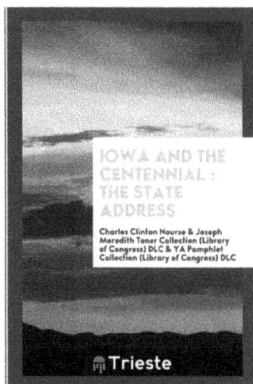

Iowa and the centennial : the state address

Unknown

ISBN: 9780649165872
Paperback: 52 pages
Dimensions: 6.14 x 0.11 x 9.21 inches
Language: eng

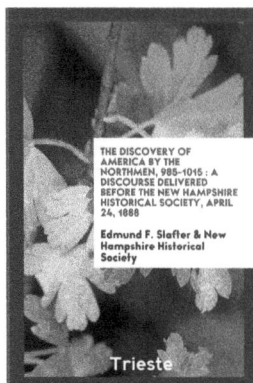

The discovery of America by the Northmen, 985-1015 : a discourse delivered before the New Hampshire Historical Society, April 24, 1888

Unknown

ISBN: 9780649166305
Paperback: 50 pages
Dimensions: 6.14 x 0.10 x 9.21 inches
Language: eng

Find more of our titles on our website. We have a selection of thousands of titles that will interest you. Please visit

www.triestepublishing.com

Lightning Source UK Ltd.
Milton Keynes UK
UKHW02f0600010618
323575UK00005B/322/P